Accepting the Troll Underneath the Bridge

Overcoming Our Self-Doubts

Terry D. Cooper

Paulist Press

New York / Mahwah, N.J.

Cover design by James F. Brisson

Cover and interior illustrations by Jon Jahraus

Interior design by Kathleen Doyle

Library of Congress Cataloging-in-Publication Data to come

Cooper, Terry D.
    Accepting the troll underneath the bridge / Terry D. Cooper.
      p.   cm.
    Includes bibliographical references.
    ISBN 0-8091-3670-8 (alk. paper)
    1. Self-acceptance–Religious aspects–Christianity. 2. Self-esteem–Religious aspects–Christianity. I. Title.
BV4647.S443066 1996
248.4–dc20

96-26387
CIP

Published by Paulist Press
997 Macarthur Boulevard
Mahwah, New Jersey 07430

Printed and bound in the
United States of America

Contents

Contents

Introduction

Perhaps you remember the fairy story, "Three Billy Goats Gruff." A prominent character in this short tale is the troll, a menacing creature who lives under a bridge and threatens anyone who attempts to cross. This brief story provides a powerful image of an internal process familiar to most of us. At some point in our lives, we attempt a transition (cross a bridge), only to be met by a heckling, ridiculing, "where-do-you-think-you're-going?" voice. The voice is demeaning, degrading, and arresting. It sometimes stops us in our tracks. It casts doubt on our ability to make it across the bridge and pushes us back to what is miserably familiar. In short, the troll is a self-sabotaging culprit who regularly abuses us. In one form or another, the troll is constantly suggesting that we are "not enough." His job is to create a suspicion of inadequacy.

Who Has a Troll Problem?

As I have introduced the image of the troll in psychology classes and educational workshops, many people have identified with this self-defeating voice of negativity. They've had troll problems, too. Of course, not everyone will admit this. In fact, if we walked up to several people and asked them how they were doing, they probably would not respond with, "Well, other than struggling with low self-esteem and an overwhelming sense of inadequacy, I'm okay." Most of us do not easily disclose our troll dilemma. Yet self-doubt gnaws and pulls at us in isolation. These feelings often provoke a need to compensate for our insecurity, so we begin to act as if we feel quite different from what we really feel. We've learned to hide our troll very well.

Consider the possibility that **all** of us struggle, to some extent, with the troll, and therefore self-acceptance is everyone's dilemma. This may help us break through some of our black-and-white thinking. For instance, perhaps we've been telling ourselves that some people possess self-esteem, while others do not. We've then divided the world into two opposing camps: those who like themselves and those who don't. When the troll raises his head, we tell ourselves we must be in the low self-esteem group. Our own troll-talk is compared with what we assume to be other people's positive self-perceptions. We can't see their troll.

The truth is that self-acceptance always seems to be a matter of degree. As new regions of ourselves are discovered, new levels of acceptance are challenged. This is an ongoing, gradual process in which self-assurance and self-doubt weave in and out. No one **totally** accepts himself or herself. While we can make progress toward greater self-acceptance, we will not "arrive" at an undisputed, serenely secure place. Even if we are quite secure today, the troll may work overtime tomorrow.

Troll Battles and Self-Obsession

If you are anything at all like me, much of your life has been an attempt to feel as if you're enough. I have spent enormous amounts of energy and effort trying to get out of the prison of self-doubt. In fact, much of my life can be marked by a series of "plans" for becoming acceptable. My drivenness was nowhere more obvious than in my frantic, psychological self-help efforts. I desperately wanted to "get" self-esteem, find my authentic self, and arrive at a state of psychological health. Personal growth became a compulsive, full-time hobby. The right workshop, book, or therapist, I believed, would surely provide deliverance.

My self-sufficiency in "finding self-esteem" quickly ran out of steam. As I tried to grant myself a verdict of acceptability, it did little good because I was the one who was on trial in the first place. It was precisely my own judgment that was being called into question. Put differently, I've been unable to psychologically save myself.

Also, the various methods by which I attempted to establish my legitimacy or "become enough" soon turned into obsessions. My focus narrowed on the salvific endeavor of becoming okay. I was consumed with conquering my troll. Psychological emancipation was in sight. My pace picked up and I worked in a frenzy.

My fixation on a plan for self-deliverance actually took the form of what religion has traditionally called idolatry. I made a god out of my own acceptability. I managed, as Thomas Oden would say, to take a finite, limited good and turn it into something pivotal for my entire existence (God).[1] It became all-consuming. It was not fueled by healthy motivation. Instead, it was driven mercilessly by an inner craving for acceptability.

One of the hardest and most humbling things for me to admit is that the door of self-doubt was not something that I could open from the inside out. God knows I tried.

Psychology offered a multitude of keys that promised to open that door, but it did not happen.

There is much literature available today which attempts to convince us that our feelings of not being enough are based on illusion. Perhaps this unfortunate conviction came from poor parenting, shaming experiences with peers or school, and so on. What we must do, we are told, is look upon this as an illusory belief. In fact, all of our problems with low self-esteem and inadequacy come from this crazy idea we've received that we're not enough. Our job is to develop the psychological muscle to reverse this conviction. In other words, in the midst of feeling unacceptable, we need to declare ourselves okay.

But what if, in the deepest layers of our experience, we have encountered the rather desperate dilemma that we really aren't enough? What if that suspicion of inadequacy is actually true? What if all the self-help efforts in the world cannot eradicate our lingering doubts? Suppose the experience of failure, of not fulfilling our deepest purposes, of somehow "falling short," reflects reality, rather than some unfortunate assumption we picked up along the way? What then?

In the midst of our deepest yearnings and failures at self-acceptance, we may find ourselves prized, accepted, and loved for the flawed people we are. My flaws are no illusion. Yet in the hopeless hours of my self-doubt, I find that my own prison is opened from the outside. None of my keys fit, but the grace of God is there anyway.

My troll, of course, has a difficult time accepting the good news that I'm acceptable in spite of my inability to rescue myself. He's mastered the message of condemnation so well that he can't (or won't) believe that the Ground and Source of all acceptance has prized him anyway. He persists in the old prison of negativity. Part of my work is to get the message of acceptance to him.

The manner may vary greatly by which we receive the message of acceptability. It can come from several sources. What's crucial, however, is that it points beyond human effort to a transcendent source of acceptance. You see, God, as I understand God, does not seem to be encumbered by the same type of ego problems I have. If I do something, I usually want immediate recognition. God, however, seems quite content to work through "messengers of acceptance" who point beyond themselves to that transforming power of Divine acceptance. Therapists, teachers, ministers, social workers, friends, and even strangers can communicate this powerful message. As Rabbi Harold Kushner frequently says in his lectures, "Human beings are God's language."

Hope for the Troll

My hope is that this book provides some helpful, healing suggestions for dealing with your troll. To accomplish this, it is necessary to understand, as clearly as possible, the troll's tricks. How does he frequently sabotage self-esteem and spoil a positive self-image? Chapter 1 explores the ways in which the troll operates.

Chapters 2, 3, and 4 look at the many attempts to sidestep or bypass the troll. The first detour is approval-seeking. The next troll-dodging maneuver is blaming and judging. The final troll evasion is aloofness and detachment. As we shall see, none of these work. These detours around the troll are related to what Karen Horney has described as three movements to escape anxiety: moving toward, moving against, and moving away from others.[2]

Chapter 5 examines how conflict exposes our troll. Various patterns or styles of handling anger are discussed and some suggestions are made for maintaining self-esteem in the face of conflict with others.

Chapter 6 suggests that, paradoxically, accepting our troll is the best way to reduce his resistance. Specific suggestions for troll acceptance are provided.

And, finally, Chapter 7 looks at the courage it takes to cross the bridge in spite of the troll underneath. Some guidelines are outlined for knowing how we are progressing.

My hope is that you find insight, comfort, and, most of all, acceptance, as you and your troll explore this book.

1.

Self-Esteem and the Troll's Tricks

Assume we are sitting in a room listening to an interesting speaker. Suppose, after about ten minutes of entertaining discussion, the speaker makes a fist and hits herself in the head, knocking herself to the floor. As she gets up to resume her speech, she talks for a couple of minutes, then clobbers herself again, this time completely knocking herself off a stool. Most of us would believe this woman to be in need of medical (probably psychiatric) help. The abuse is apparent. This self-inflicted pain needs some sort of intervention. Why would she attack and victimize her own being? What a strange way to treat herself.

Yet the above scene is precisely what occurs in the thinking process of many of us. We may not beat ourselves physically, but we brutalize ourselves mentally. How? By exaggerated criticisms, condemnations, self-judgments, and generalizations. We magnify our flaws and completely blow things out of proportion. We start an avalanche of verbal self-abuse. We may not talk out loud when this is going on, but the battering still occurs sub-vocally. A snickering, heckling, demeaning voice comments on our shortcomings. Our troll is active. Mistakes are interpreted as failures. Being uninformed is labeled as "stupid." The troll feeds on the hype of emotionally-charged language. He is a master at name-calling. In short, he turns us into our own worst enemy.

It's very important for us to become as familiar as we can with our troll. While his style may vary a little from person to person, his primary character remains the same. His main vocation is to do nothing except hang out under a bridge and criticize any meaningful movement toward achievement, growth, and mental health. "Who do you think you are?" "You'll never be able to accomplish that!" "Get back to where it's safe." The bridge, which represents change and growth, is the target of the troll's heckling comments. His task is to create self-doubt and keep me from taking a risk. The troll does not want me to attempt the unfamiliar. He's always against stretching my limits. He's cynical, sarcastic, and self-defeating. Again, the troll does not **do** anything. His whole point is to stop activity. He spreads negativity like a wicked virus. He attempts to poison motivation and keep me locked in a fearful state of life. Afraid to hope, the troll is quite skeptical of change. Personal growth, he believes, is a futile endeavor. We are what we are—stuck, condemned, and doomed to live out the lives handed to us. The troll works better in the dark. He lives in the shadows of exaggeration. He uses the irrational to attack us. When we truly see the way he functions in our lives, we are halfway home.

We can hear the troll in many people's comments. The forty-eight-year-old woman who is going back to college after being out of school for over twenty years may hear, "Do you know how silly you look?" "Are you trying to be a teenager again?" "You'll never learn this." "You'd better stick to what you know." The ridiculing, limiting voice of the troll keeps her fenced into low self-esteem. The troll encourages her to stay with the familiar, even when it makes her unhappy.

A fifty-year-old man, undergoing a second divorce, begins to connect his current behavior to abuse issues in his childhood. As he becomes excited over changing his patterns of behavior, the troll begins: "You can't change." "You're stuck!" "You are what you are." "The past is too powerful." "Your life's been ruined, so face it!"

Again, other people may have different images of this internal, self-defeating voice. The common thread in all these images appears to be the antagonistic and demeaning nature of this internal enemy. The voices ambush us, indict us, and keep us frozen in unhealthy attitudes and behavior. The troll robs us of growth. Common messages sound like this:

I'm unattractive.
I'm stupid.
I'm not well liked.

6

I'm never even noticed.
I'm too emotional.
I'm boring.
I'm inadequate.
I'm inferior.
I'm too insecure.
I have no confidence.
I'm ashamed of myself.
I don't know how to have any fun.
I'm too shy.
I'm self-centered.
I'm irresponsible.
I'm immature.
I'm just a coward.
I'm lazy.
I've failed in all my relationships.
Nobody understands me.
I can't take criticism.
I don't make enough money.
I'm afraid to live.
What if I'm wrong?
What will they think of me?
I'll never fit in.
I could **never** work there.
I could **never** learn that.
I can't change.
I'm a psychological mess.
I'm a weak person.
What if I fail?
What if I succeed?
Everyone expects too much!
My feelings will destroy me.
No one can get along with me.
I'm completely disorganized.
I'm not lovable.
I'm hopeless.

These negative messages hound, heckle, and distort our clear thinking about ourselves. Their function is to condemn, not to inform. The troll's task is wrecking self-confidence and keeping us within narrow restraints.

Notice the way these internal statements attack us rather than our behavior. These fiery indictments are thrown at our being, our identity, our sense of worth. The troll is uninterested in the modest task of pointing toward specific behavior that could be changed. That's not dramatic enough. That's too limited in scope. He is hungry for an assault. Why concentrate on a specific habit or behavior when he can rage against the entire self? Why pass up a chance to be judgmental?

The troll's strategy is the "oversimplify and insult" plan. He divides the world into all-or-nothing categories, then places us in the negative group. We are either good or bad, compassionate or unfeeling, warm or cold, genuine or phony, hard-working or lazy, intelligent or stupid. Having made these tidy polar opposites, the troll then slams us into the unattractive category.

During rational moments, most of us are unable to classify ourselves in the troll's all-or-nothing scheme. We know that life is more complicated than that. We also recognize that we are somewhat different in every situation. It is unrealistic to say we are "always," "completely," "totally," "absolutely," "simply," or "just" any-thing. We're more complex than that.

Yet the troll tries to reduce our experience, polarize our behavior, then condemn us to the "bad" group. He reminds us of our inadequacy during moments of weakness, and convinces us that all so-called mysteries and complications within us are mere cover-ups for our depravity.

Troll Beginnings

It is tempting, though rarely possible, to track down the origins of the troll. Where did he come from? How did he develop such sarcasm and negativity? How did life create such an ugly creature? How did our thinking become so self-belittling and judgmental?

The troll seems to operate his own collection agency of condemnations. He has gathered every possible negative, shaming, critical message over the years. All the condemning voices from the outside now have an inside representative. A raging parent, for instance, no longer has to be present. The troll has taken over the job and we've learned to rage at ourselves. A humiliating teacher no longer has to suggest that we are stupid. Our own troll is happy to replay the old tape with a new level of intensity.

When the Troll Uses Religion

Sometimes the troll turns theologian. His voice can seem so powerful that we become convinced that he reflects some sort of ultimate reality. In other words, we can confuse his debilitating messages with "the voice of God." When this happens, we've given the troll religious endorsement and sanctioned his abuse. We have called something "holy" when its entire mission is self-destruction. Perhaps we've told ourselves that God thinks we're "worthless, stupid, totally irresponsible, wicked," and so on. The troll's judgments have been handed over to the Divine. Because we think we are vile, God must see us this way, too. The inner pronouncements against us must surely emerge from an ultimate source. They should be taken at face value and not questioned. Our depravity comes from a cosmic verdict, not just our own exaggerated opinion. Our self-hatred receives a divine reinforcement. We are quite disgusted with ourselves, so we project that disgust onto God.

The troll loves to "hide out" in a religious disguise. He thrives on the business of holy hatred, especially self-hatred. After all, we are far less likely to expose his roots when we attribute him to God. Our shame is heightened. Condemnation is expanded. Fear has turned us into a passive victim of sadistic superstition.

Our troll, then, can control our image of God. Unfortunately, that image looks very much like the troll. God becomes demanding, relentless, reactionary, shaming, irrational, and out to get us. This God is not easy to "warm up to." In fact, fear prevents any sort of intimacy with this picture of God. Who **could** like him? And this is precisely the dilemma in which many people find themselves: they insist on worshiping a God they don't even like. Once again, who can feel affection for a Tyrant poised and ready to blast us with judgment? Who wants to get close to cosmic abuse? Who needs it?

When self-hatred is stamped with religious approval, it becomes much more difficult to challenge and change. It's hard for us to believe in ourselves when we think God can't stand us. Because the Cosmic Parent disapproves, the indictment immobilizes us. It's extremely important to "smoke out" the self-destructive voice of the troll and realize that it has to do with us, not God.

Shame—The Troll's Weapon

The troll likes shame much more than guilt. In fact, he thrives on turning guilt into shame. Guilt, if it is healthy, has a limited, instructional function. It points toward the need to align our behavior with our beliefs. An inconsistency is occurring, and guilt invites examination. Sometimes our behavior needs to be changed. At other times, our beliefs or expectations are unrealistic and need to be adjusted. The point is that when it is functioning in a healthy manner, we need not be afraid of guilt. It can serve as a friend, a guide, a helper in living out the kind of lives we deeply want.

A healthy sense of guilt is too modest for the troll's purposes. Therefore, he works on converting it to shame. When this happens, it's not our behavior that is being examined. Instead, **we** are on trial. The troll, as inward prosecutor, brings evidence against our very being. Shame carries with it the conviction that something very basic or essential is wrong with us. Guilt, like fire, is a useful tool for maintaining our lives. Shame pours gasoline on the fire. Toxic shame does nothing to instruct, encourage, or motivate. It serves absolutely no practical function. It is the troll's ugly fascination with self-destruction.

The Troll's "Dirty Dozen"

The self-sabotaging antics of the troll are based on a shrewd strategy for maintaining low self-esteem. These tricks can be summarized around the word CONDEMNATION.

C ompulsively compare yourself unfavorably with others
O bsess constantly on "how you are coming across"
N ag at yourself for your low self-esteem
D evelop victim-thinking: external things control you
E quate self-confidence with arrogance and conceit
M ake self-esteem an isolated, fix-it-at-home ordeal
N ever separate what you can and cannot change
A llow perfectionism to go unchecked
T ie feelings of worth to external signs of success
I gnore yourself by projecting on others
O vershadow insecurity by dominating and controlling
N ever challenge a horrifying imagination

Let's look a little more thoroughly at each one of these troll tricks.

Trick #1—Compulsively compare ourselves unfavorably with others. The troll wants us to measure our inner insecurity with other people's outer display of security. We begin to match our worst against their best. We assume that others never have confidence problems such as ours. If they appear calm on the outside, we automatically believe they must be equally calm on the inside. The result is always feeling as if others have something we do not.

Trick #2—Obsess constantly on how we are coming across. The troll wants us to worry incessantly about how we appear. He whispers that people are always watching and evaluating us. Every move we make is under the scrutiny of critical eyes. Other people are as critical of us as we are of ourselves. We thus develop the feeling that we are always on stage, under pressure, and being assessed. Our self-absorption is encouraged as we worry about what "they" think. We don't relax or enjoy the freedom of self-abandon. There is too much on the line for that! We must remember that we are always leaving someone with an impression.

The troll especially encourages us to focus and obsess on all our mistakes and inadequacies. He collects and connects scenes from past failures and periodically shows them to us. He tell us that everyone sees how ridiculous we appear. Ruminate, recycle, and wallow, he says, in things we regret. Tell ourselves that we've ruined our lives. See mistakes as fatal. Obsess on what went wrong, why we did what we did, and what we wish we would have done differently. Endlessly dig up the same soil of discontentment. We fouled up! We must punish ourselves with a daily reminder of it. How could we have done this? What in the world got into our heads?

We then begin to put all our energies into figuring out our wrong moves. We never concentrate on what we learned from the experience. The fact that we may have gained a great deal of inner strength goes unnoticed. Nor do we consider how this episode may have given us greater compassion for others in similar predicaments. The pain may have made us more human, but we fixate on how we messed up. As our "disaster" is remembered, we shake our heads in shame, roll our eyes, and feel embarrassed all over again. In fact, we re-experience the entire situation when the topic comes up. No sympathy is allowed for our mistake. We refuse to put the event in psychological context and see the multitude of situational factors that prompted our decision. No excuses! There is no point in trying to get ourselves off the hook with a lot of wishy-washy situational thinking. Just remember that we blew it, and that's that.

Trick #3—Nag at ourselves for our low self-esteem. The troll encourages us to get down on ourselves for being down on ourselves! After all, we know how important self-esteem is, so how could we allow ourselves to get in this shape? The troll wants to go beyond merely acknowledging low self-esteem. Instead, we should beat ourselves up for having the problem. After all, we ought to be farther along. We ought to be embarrassed by our lack of confidence. Our self-image is weak and pitiful. Why didn't we develop inner strength along the way?

When we "abuse ourselves because we abuse ourselves," we create a vicious cycle of intolerance and judgment. We would not seriously consider beating our leg because it is broken. Yet the troll often berates us for our own low opinion of ourselves.

Trick #4—Develop victim thinking: external things control us. The troll encourages victim thinking by telling us that outside events, things, and people control our feelings. He insists that forces outside of us determine what is inside of us. This reinforces the belief that we can't really do anything about our situation. "It" (life, people, circumstances) regulates our happiness and controls what we think and feel. Our world is one big stimulus-response experiment. We "get" provoked, are "made" angry, and "forced" to be sad. The power is always external. We are emotionally stuck with whatever happens. We can complain about it, but we can't change it. Someone's snide remark, for instance, may hurt our feelings for days. Or we may automatically punch someone for calling us a name. After finding out that a neighbor made some sarcastic comments about us, we may obsess on it for days. Perhaps we become easily intimidated around an intellectual colleague. Or we may feel inferior whenever a wealthy person comes into our home.

Believing that these external factors control us will whittle away any sense of personal power, independence, or self-direction. Our self-esteem will be deeply wounded by this chronic belief that we are a slave of our own predicament. The situation will take us hostage and we will have no real voice in the matter. We can only react.

Reacting is demeaning, while choosing is empowering. When we tell ourselves that we must react in a particular way, we insult our humanness. By denying our options, we deny our dignity. It's the ability to rise above the reactive impulse, pause, and choose our response that promotes self-respect and dignity. The troll wants us to see ourselves without alternatives.

The troll believes other people have the power to validate or invalidate our sense of worth. Our self-esteem is in their hands. We are allowed to accept ourselves when, and only when, other people like us. If they don't like us, something must be wrong with us. Their opinion becomes the barometer for what we think of ourselves.

The troll also wants us to be the victims of abusive relationships (physically, emotionally, spiritually, and financially). Not protecting ourselves against abuse will do enormous damage to our self-esteem. We'll soon believe we don't deserve protection. We'll also assume we don't have the ability to stand up for ourselves. Passively allowing our rights to be violated will deteriorate our spirit and self-respect. Staying with a physically or emotionally violent relationship, continuing with a job that involves daily insults from a boss, constantly "footing the bill" for a friend out of money, allowing someone to tell us that our religious views are totally off base—all these things erode self-care.

Another variation of this trick is proclaiming that if we had a bad childhood, low self-esteem is inevitable. We're stuck with inferiority feelings for life. They are a part of an unchangeable personality structure, and there is nothing we can do about it. These negative messages simply cannot be unlearned. We can never replace what was missing back there. We must accept our fate.

Trick #5—Equate self-confidence with arrogance and conceit. The troll does not want us to focus, even for a moment, on what we do well or may like about ourselves. We must prohibit any acknowledgement of our assets. This would be egotistical foolishness and self-indulgence. Once we start getting too high on ourselves, we are headed for a fall. So, we must refuse to admit our strengths, and stay focused on what is lacking in us. This will keep us humble and protect us from the terrors of pride. Modesty means seeing ourselves in a lowly manner.

Even when someone compliments us, we shouldn't allow it into our awareness. Discount it. Minimize it. Say, "Oh, that's nothing." If people like our hair, we can tell them that we really need to have it cut. If people like a shirt or blouse, tell them that we could stand to lose some weight. If people say we are pleasant, tell them they don't see us during the mornings. If we are told we cooked an excellent meal, mention that the rolls were nearly burnt. Find ways of blocking, denying, or at least "watering down" any positive statements about us.

After a while, our negative self-image can function like a comfortable prison. It's safe to stay within the secure world of having no talents, possessing no abilities, and having no dreams. We won't have to worry about seeing new possibilities. If we have nothing to offer, we have nothing to lose. We can creep along at a snail's pace, stagnant and afraid. Seeing our strengths would lead to a burden, namely, what to do with them! The troll says we had better stay where we are.

Trick #6—Make self-esteem an isolated, fix-it-at-home ordeal. The troll insists that we view self-esteem as a completely private matter. We need not have support resources. Instead, we must change our self-image in isolation. The bridge must be crossed alone. Our self-image must heroically change through our own unaided effort. Thus, the troll grooms emotional hermits. We sit at home alone and read books on self-confidence, expecting to transform our self-concept without the benefit of others. We are probably too embarrassed to tell anyone else where we're really at, anyway.

Again, the troll's motto is: self-sufficiency in all matters of self-improvement. We must do it ourselves! This is too private and personal to share. Inner strength will simply appear! We do not need to connect with friends, groups, workshops, or church to help fuel our self-esteem. There's no need to become vulnerable. Put on a solid front and work on self-esteem issues in private.

Trick #7—Never separate what we can and cannot change. Instead, we should try to change "the world" and "other people" without ever looking at ourselves. We should beat our heads against a wall of frustration as we attempt to rehabilitate others. We should try to control them, overextending ourselves with the task of transforming people. Then, after we've failed, we can fall on our faces.

If we have a dinner party, for instance, we should feel responsible if someone becomes even slightly bored. If we suggest a particular movie, we should blame ourselves if someone does not like it. We may expect ourselves to persuasively convince someone to quit taking drugs. Or we may consider it our mission to "make" someone more open-minded. As a consequence, we'll get so bogged down in what we cannot change that we'll have no energy left for the things we can change.

Trick #8—Allow perfectionism to go unchecked. The troll rigorously puts us down for not achieving an impossible standard. He makes a romanticized, inflated image of what we "should" be the measuring stick for our self-esteem. When we don't match what the image says we ought to be, he harshly condemns us. We should feel and think only what this perfect standard tells us. For instance, if the standard says we must never feel angry, we should shame ourselves when this feeling emerges. We will then refuse to accept the full range of our emotions. After all, our perfect image has narrow parameters of what we are allowed to feel. We must stay within this framework. In fact, if a feeling falls outside of this framework, we may want to tell ourselves that the feeling is simply not real. Or perhaps we could rename the feeling. We could call our anger "just being concerned," or refer to our rage as "caring a lot." By renaming our feelings, we can stay within the strict guidelines of our all-important image. Our "prescribed self" can remain intact. If we do this long enough, we won't even realize we are deceiving ourselves. We'll feel what we're "supposed" to feel. And what we are supposed to feel will drown out anything real. Our standard will control our awareness. We'll censor, deny, or minimize anything that falls outside of our guidelines.

The troll also has rules about "perfect" confidence. We must attempt nothing until we have complete self-assurance. If we don't feel secure, we shouldn't try something. We must wait on "confidence." This "confidence" will be a magical, transforming event making us totally self-assured. **Then** we will be okay; **now** we'd better wait. Self-esteem is thus turned into something we will suddenly "get." It is lurking out there in the future.

As we passively wait on this mythological moment of complete confidence, we'll do nothing with our lives. Our assumption that confidence must precede action actually puts the cart ahead of the horse. Confidence follows, rather than precedes, our efforts. The troll does not want us to notice this. It's when we take a risk, try something new, or move ahead even though we're not sure of ourselves, that confidence is developed. It comes as a result of faith. Yet the troll insists we must have an appearance of full assurance before we start anything.

Trick #9—Tie feelings of worth to external signs of success. The troll wants to convince us that all feelings of worth are attached to signs of social success

15

(money, prestige, or popularity). There is no need to question the priorities of our culture. We **are** what we **have**! We must not forget this. And what we "have" is all on the outside. It is what we can show others. Our worth is tied to our ability to impress. Self-esteem rests on the quality of our houses, number of automobiles, association with well-known people, and financial status. We should accept, at face value, these factors as measures of success. Success has nothing to do with what is inside of us. After all, we can't show that to anyone. If we can't put something on display, it must not be worth much.

Trick # 10—Ignore ourselves by projecting on others. The troll never owns up to anything he can blame on someone else. He says we can distract from ourselves by focusing on other people's faults. If we start to become aware of our own problems, throw the spotlight onto others. Use **them** to avoid **us**. Take their inventory. The minute we become even slightly uncomfortable with ourselves, shift to the outside. Blast away at their problems. Over-react, if necessary, in order to keep attention away from ourselves.

Trick #11—Overshadow insecurity by dominating and controlling. The troll wants to demonstrate our "lack" of insecurity by dominating others in continual power struggles. All relationships are competitive, and we must win. We have to prove to others that we are not weak. People will push us around if we let them, so aggression is necessary to get ahead. We must show our superiority. This may mean arguing until we convince others of our point of view. It may mean bullying, badgering, or intimidating. Compromise is weak. We'll prove our strength, and after enough times perhaps we'll also convince ourselves.

Trick #12—Never challenge a horrifying imagination. This final trick in the troll's dozen is his unlimited ability to imagine how awful failure would be. He wants us to live with an overblown image of potential devastation. In fact, we should allow our fear of failure to dominate us. The troll creates a landscape of horror. He constantly imagines that some dreadful fate could befall us. Anxiety-ridden fantasies keep us right where we are—stuck in low self-esteem.

These, then, are the troll's "dirty dozen." As we begin to recognize them, the troll will no doubt become frustrated. He is accustomed to working in the dark with few challenges. Understanding his tricks is the first vital step toward making it across the bridge.

2.

Approval-Seeking: "Out-Pleasing" Our Troll

One of the most obvious cover-ups for self-doubt is approval-seeking. We seek, as a way of life, other people's endorsement, approval, and validation. What others think becomes the guiding force in our lives. Our constant concern is how our behavior will affect someone else. We do things that will be pleasing, voice opinions in agreement with others, and stay within the boundaries of someone's favor. We'll "out-please" the troll's voice. Surely this will keep the troll away from us. Thus, our lives will not be lived from the **inside out**. Instead, they'll flow from the **outside in**. We'll read and evaluate our performance from other people's faces, comments, and reactions. Our self-esteem will be in their hands. Naturally, this will create enormous anxiety. After all, our acceptability will be continuously in front of an examining board. Their opinions matter, ours do not; their feelings are significant, ours are irrelevant; their perception of us must be accurate, while we know little of ourselves.

This approval-seeking attempt to dodge the troll has put us in a most precarious position. The sad fact is that we easily abandon ourselves as we focus on outside reactions. Other people "dispense" grace to us and we seek it like starved creatures. We elevate their opinion to a godlike status and painfully ignore our own.

Approval-seeking and self-abandonment are actually two sides of the same coin. Both assume that someone else's opinion is better simply because it is someone else's. Because nothing inside of us counts, we must find something outside of us for validation. Consequently, we believe we cannot depend on ourselves for an accurate picture of who we are. Others must have some secret information or inside dope on us. Our "self-assessment apparatus" is faulty and defective. We are untrustworthy interpreters of our own experience. Eagerly, we look to others to tell us what we mean, what we've experienced, and what we're all about. Unfortunately, there are plenty of people quite ready to offer their expert advice on who we are. These outsiders may have never felt our feelings, understood our past, or appreciated the struggles of our experience. Yet we allow them to tell us what we "should do" and "ought to have done." Further, we give them power to decide the way we see ourselves. Their opinion defines us. Our hunger for outside confirmation sets us up to be under their authority.

JoAnn's Story of Approval-Seeking

Consider, for example, JoAnn. JoAnn had always feared any thought of being selfish, self-centered, or, God forbid, self-indulgent. Most of her life had been spent trying to anticipate and manage other people's feelings and reactions. She had become good at it. A single parent, she had learned to juggle work outside the home with the kids' schedules. She usually felt her children's feelings even before they felt them. And naturally, she felt responsible for those feelings. Still troubled about the effects of a "failed marriage," she took full responsibility for her children's happiness. Her self-image was intricately tied to what her kids thought.

JoAnn carried these same tendencies into her job as a manager. She had a boss with limited interpersonal skills, little patience, and low frustration tolerance. He owned his own restaurant and was quite difficult to approach. Employees found him moody, temperamental, and non-affirming. He was hard to please.

The pivotal person, of course, was JoAnn. She felt responsible for keeping her boss from being grumpy, responsible for keeping her staff content and motivated, and responsible for keeping customers feeling the warmth of a hospitable restaurant. She was the rescuer in a dangerous triangle. Her boss (the villain!) displayed unhealthy behavior in front of the staff (the victims) for which she had to compensate. She had to "cover his tracks" and keep peace between "daddy and the kids." The restaurant looked more and more like a disturbed family. JoAnn protected the owner's image, telling

18

employees, "he didn't really mean it," "he's just under a lot of stress," or "you know how he gets." JoAnn always had excuses available for him, and sought approval he was incapable of giving. She continued to stuff her feelings over his many insensitivities. JoAnn minimized his unhealthy behavior because she minimized her own feelings and rights.

Claiming responsibility for others' feelings, JoAnn measured herself by her ability to keep peace, cheer everyone up, make her kids happy, keep her employees content, and listen (like a counselor!) to her customers. She worried constantly about everyone else's feelings, and once again saw those feelings as a direct commentary on her. She took, as gospel, other people's opinion of her. She was devastated by criticism, and would go to any length to win a favorable impression.

Eventually, JoAnn ran out of steam. She became depressed, lost energy, cried daily, and felt like giving up. Life had become an obligation, a burden, a curse. It was only when JoAnn started becoming aware of her self-avoidance that she began to regain strength. The beautiful person she was had been neglected and abandoned long ago. She had much sadness and anger about selling out to herself. She became outraged about the number of people she had put on a pedestal as more important than she. She began to see lifelong patterns of approval-seeking. Vacations, support groups, and self-care became part of JoAnn's commitment. JoAnn discovered that caring for others need not exclude taking care of herself. In fact, she started realizing that self-care is essential if she is to have anything to give others. She sought out friends with whom she could be herself. She began to let other people handle their own conflicts. She quit

19

enabling her boss, and let him take responsibility for the image he left employees. As JoAnn acknowledged her inability to control what anyone thinks about her, she discovered an oasis of energy.

Some Helpful Hints for Approval-Seekers

The hard part for approval-seekers is breaking away from the quick fix. When we become self-doubting, old patterns automatically pop up, and before we know it our self-esteem is in someone else's hands again. It may be bumpy at first, but we can survive rejection and learn to appreciate ourselves in the face of opposition. The initial experience **will** hurt. We will doubt ourselves. Others will resist our change in outlook. Yet the inner freedom we gain is certainly worth our struggle.

Let's look at some important points to remember about our need for approval. First, approval is nice but not necessary. We're kidding ourselves when we say we don't care at all what others think. When outsiders offer compliments, most of us like it. We enjoy the favorable opinions of others. Yet we run into problems when we say that their approval is essential or necessary. A desire is one thing; a demand is quite another. We will not emotionally, spiritually, or physically die from anyone's disapproval. We can certainly survive in the face of negative input. In fact, we already live with disapproval; we just may not know about it yet.

Some people believe they are unhealthy simply because they still want or like approval. Yet enjoying approval is completely natural and humanly inevitable. Disapproval, regardless of how healthy we become, stings. The point is not to become devastated, controlled, or even strongly affected by it. In short, we should not hand disapproval over to the troll. He will make mincemeat of us. He will turn external disapproval into internal disapproval. When the troll smashes us with other people's comments, it is because we have already orphaned ourselves.

Second, we have many sources of acceptance available to us. There are many pockets of acceptance, nurture, and encouragement. The trouble begins when we think we must have the acceptance and approval of any one particular person or group. This becomes idolatry, as we elevate a limited opinion to a godlike status. Many wells are accessible, so we need not keep going back to empty ones. No particular group has a monopoly on the acceptance business.

Positive, healthy affirmation refuels our belief in ourselves. The way others see

20

us "matches" the acceptance we wish to offer ourselves. These groups encourage, rather than discourage, self-trust. While they cannot "give us" self-esteem, they can certainly help refuel it. It is easy to ignore these clusters of acceptance and obsess on one particular unaccepting target. We may even have the support of many, but we easily discount their acceptance. Friends, a support group, church members, work associates, and many others may care for us. Yet the troll wants us to exclusively focus on that distant, non-affirming person or group, and make all other forms of acceptance irrelevant. We want what they cannot give. The positive qualities others see in us are minimized or denied. With a narrow, relentless focus, we care only about the mythologized, deified opinion of this unaccepting source.

Third, obsession with others' approval means that we disrespect ourselves. Not listening to, paying attention to, or trusting ourselves involves a profound sense of disrespect. This is a form of saying, "All things valuable are outside of me." As we desperately chase the approval of others, we step right over our own opinion. The result is becoming deaf to our own inner voice, a stranger to our own convictions.

Why do we automatically assume that someone else's perspective is superior to our own? How does this inferiority spring up so easily? Why do we not value the perceptions of the one who has been with us all along—ourselves. Yet another's angle, however limited may be their knowledge of us, is often respected more than we respect ourselves. This is a sad commentary on our inner life.

Fourth, disapproval is often the price we pay for being ourselves. It is important to remember that honesty will indeed bring unfortunate responses. If no one disapproves of us, the overwhelming likelihood is that we're not being real. Genuine people are not always liked. We need this reminder as a reality check. Disapproval does **not** mean that something is wrong with us, nor that we cannot get along with others. A certain amount of accumulated disapproval follows anyone committed to an authentic, open, self-loyal life.

Fifth, no amount of outside approval can ever resolve an inside problem. This is perhaps the hardest lesson of life to learn. Many of us constantly seek that final, once-and-for-all confirmation of our worth. We may take different roads to find this secure place, but emptiness quickly returns as we experience more false promises. We cannot **do** enough to solve a **being** problem. Life becomes an endless attempt to justify our existence.

It is odd that this is such a difficult lesson for most of us. Our need to earn acceptance compulsively drives us until we're worn down. We switch from one path to another. If professors think we are smart enough, neighbors think we are wealthy enough, co-workers think we are professional enough, partners think we are sexy enough, psychologists think we are "together" enough, and ministers think we are holy enough, then we'll be okay. Yet this approval hunger is never satisfied. We simply cannot become content on the basis of outside validation. No amount of endorsement can provide self-acceptance.

Sixth, the need for approval often leaves us indecisive. There are many conflicting people to please. When we cannot count on ourselves for direction, we go through inner turmoil, frustration, and confusion as we listen to others. Because there are so many voices, we often wander aimlessly trying to decide which one to follow. Many people will have opinions about what kind of car we should buy, whom we should date, where we should attend church, where we should go to school, or how we should spend our day. Opinions are abundant and, without a trust in ourselves, overwhelming. Careful thinking and the consideration of outside opinion is one thing; attempting to please every advice-happy person we know is quite another. Indecisiveness often results from a lack of confidence in our ability to handle a confusing situation, face stress, and choose for ourselves.

Seventh, when we desperately need the approval of others, we set ourselves up for being manipulated by them. When we need others' approval, they have power over us. This power can be used against us. They may withhold affection, make demands, invade our privacy, or put us down. Because we need their approval so badly, we do not challenge or confront them. They have the fix we need, so the relationship is already out of balance. They have a secret weapon available—our neediness. We simply need their approval too much to be honest.

Eighth, when we desperately need approval, we tend to overreact to any criticism. When approval becomes too important, we handicap ourselves from constructively handling criticism. We tend to react in one of two ways: (a) we automatically accept all criticism at face value, or (b) we become explosive and defensive. In either case, too much power is given to others' comments.

Some of us approval-seekers become devastated by criticism because we immediately believe negative comments are valid. We have a readiness to believe the worst about ourselves. Our sense of adequacy is shaky, so we easily believe the unfavorable impression is accurate.

Other approval-seekers violently react to criticism, obsess on it, fight it, and spend enormous energy defending themselves against it. When we take this approach, we are still granting the criticism undeserved power. It indirectly controls us the whole time we fight it. When we "must prove" we are not the way others say, then "what they say" has controlling power.

And, finally, changing approval-seeking habits takes practice. We may have significant insights into our approval-seeking, understand how we became this way, and recognize what this interpersonal habit has cost us. The solution to our problem, however, is in practicing a different way of life. Each time we face disapproval and remain loyal to ourselves, we gain inner confidence and strength. This is something we must do, not just something we think or feel. A change in behavior then reinforces our thinking and we recognize the futility of chasing what we don't need. Until this time, we may know it in our heads, but it has not yet become a gut-level reality.

All change begins with awareness and assessment. Where has our approval-seeking gotten us? Well liked? Sometimes. Respected? Probably not. Most likely, others will not respect us until we respect ourselves. And all self-respect begins with paying attention. Paying attention to whom? Ourselves. This does not mean "cosmetic attention." And it does not mean "let's-impress-others" attention. Instead, we offer ourselves a peaceful, private attention that encourages growth. The troll does not know how to deal with this. It means noticing what we like, dislike, think, hope, dread, and hate. This is the first step toward self-respect. We can learn to await, like expectant parents, what emerges within us. We don't have to escape our troll by pleasing everyone. In fact, we don't have the energy for it.

3.

Blaming and Judging: Projecting Our Troll

Judging, blaming, and harshly criticizing others appears to have little to do with low self-esteem or a lack of self-acceptance. After all, we judgmental and critical people are often loud, overbearing, dominating, arrogant and abusive. We do not look at all like the insecure approval-seekers previously discussed. Instead, we appear to be **too** self-assured, always right, and never to blame. We have a built-in ability to excuse ourselves from all mistakes and a keen ability to find fault outside ourselves.

When we cannot admit mistakes and accept our human errors, we feel psychological pressure to locate all faults outside of ourselves. Any internal problem must be externalized. Of necessity, we must explain our problems on the basis of other people's behavior. Perpetual excuses are made to keep our image pure. It's **their** fault. **They** are to blame. Some villain outside of us is at work again. Blaming becomes the backbone of our refusal to emotionally grow up and be responsible for our lives.

Judgmentalism in Action—Warren's Story

Consider Warren. Warren had been quick to judge what he thought was inappropriate, immoral, "sinful" behavior. He prided himself on being able to "call it like it is." He frequently talked about how morally wishy-washy and religiously indifferent people were becoming. Warren thought he shouldn't hesitate to take a stand, denounce ungodliness, protest what was unclean in his community, and so on. His troll was quite active in his disdain for others.

Warren understood his attitude as simply having strong convictions. He wanted to reflect a perfect image of holiness, which he completely tied to moral purity. He gained his identity from what he denounced, rebuked, and morally judged. His feelings of moral superiority, grandiosity, and self-righteousness were all hidden behind his religious convictions. He was "God's man."

Warren also saw his family's behavior as a direct reflection of his level of holiness. They, too, must convey an impeccable image. He monitored his wife's behavior and had frequent criticisms if she "got out of line." Occasionally, she would get angry, which in and of itself worried Warren. But then she would use foul language! He constantly parented her about her word choice. In fact, Warren was **everyone's** conscience. This was a marvelous way of avoiding his own troll.

His controlling tendencies (under the banner of religion) also stretched to his kids. Todd, an adolescent son, was the primary target. Warren felt enormous anxiety about Todd's puberty experience. Todd's sexuality, his enjoyment of rock and roll music, and his growing desire for privacy (all part of the adolescent package) were scrutinized and exaggerated by Warren. In fact, Warren made most everything in Todd's life his business. He obsessed on what Todd might be doing because he refused to face regions of his own dark side. There was much within Warren that he refused to investigate, much less accept. He chronically projected his own troll onto Todd. It was Todd, he told himself, who was flooded with sexual thoughts, rebellion, defiance, and anger.

The more controlling Warren became, the more resistant was Todd. One of the ways Todd expressed his rebellion was through smoking pot. Gradually Todd became involved with other chemicals as well. Marijuana, prescription diet pills, tranquilizers,

cocaine, and alcohol became nonjudgmental friends to a teenager from a very judgmental family.

Eventually, Warren found out about Todd's activities and exploded. After a series of violent confrontations in which Warren beat his son (again, in the name of God), Todd attempted suicide. At the hospital, Todd was placed in the chemical dependency unit, and the full range of his using habits was discovered.

Todd's parents were encouraged to participate in the hospital's family program. Initially, Warren's dominant feeling was shame. But this was not the shame of having neglected his son. Instead, it was the shame of having his image tarnished. How could such a godly man be put through this? He would be forced to associate with drug addicts and irresponsible parents. He would have to spend several weekends with the "degenerate" side of life.

Warren's self-righteous attitudes and moral superiority were rigorously challenged in the family program. The bulk of this challenge came from a hospital chaplain who talked about (and modeled) compassion, owning our responsibility in family dysfunction, and accepting others where they are. This chaplain did not use a lot of traditional religious language, but there was a down-to-earth power about his manner. He was real, and everyone knew it.

Initially, Warren was defensive, stubborn, and authoritarian. However, one Saturday afternoon, a seventeen-year-old girl got to him. April, a teenager Warren had never seen, began to talk about her own family. She had progressively gotten involved with drugs and made some choices she regretted. She had become pregnant, and did not know what to do.

Scared and desperately needing love, she went to her father. Tears flowed like glistening spirits from April's eyes when she described how her father said he wanted "nothing to do with a whore." He said April was "not his daughter," and literally kicked her out of the house.

Something within the honest spirit of this seventeen-year-old touched Warren. Usually unemotional, Warren felt the liberating tears of self-awareness fall down his cheeks. He saw himself mirrored in April's father. He hugged his son, and told him that he would love him "no matter what."

As Warren worked further in the family program and participated in follow-up counseling, he realized that his rigid, hyperreligious, judgmental attitude was a cover-up for a painful childhood. Warren had been extremely embarrassed by his alcoholic, womanizing father. The pendulum had swung too far in the opposite direction as Warren promised himself that his life would be full of holiness instead of booze and sex. He had covered his pain with a righteous veneer. He had not allowed himself to express and process the fear, hurt, and shame of his past. He was running away from himself in the name of God.

Becoming Less Judgmental

It is very frightening to drop our blaming mask and look in the mirror. What will we find? Will we survive after the inventory? Can we admit our mistakes without feeling "defined" by those mistakes? A shaky, fragile, troll-based self-image will be too scared to explore very far. Living under the threat of excessive judgment pushes us to the outer world. The fault must be found **out there** because it is too painful to locate it **in here**. Blaming is thus a primary way of running away from ourselves. When we're blaming others, we are actually eliminating the possibility of self-knowledge.

Firing away at the enemy "out there" keeps us away from inward discoveries. We actually need these culprits to escape ourselves. What would we do with no one to blame?

Blaming, then, is a stubborn block to self-ownership. We must recognize, admit, and accept shortcomings as our own if we are to move beyond them. Any person or group that encourages blaming, either directly or indirectly, is an obstacle to healthy living. When we blame others, we sink deeper into a victim role. Blaming is born out of weakness, not strength. It has no vision, no hope, no motivation. It is giving up. It is allowing the power in our lives to be somewhere other than within us.

Blaming also poisons our relationships. Balance, fairness, perspective-taking, negotiating, and responsibility are wiped out in a blizzard of critical accusations. It's always someone else who creates our mood, causes our behavior, makes us react, hurts our feelings, ruins our day, or upsets us. We assume a passive, victim status and claim that others have contaminated, controlled, and disabled us. How awful they are!

Recognizing our mistakes actually brings a liberating and relaxing willingness to be human. We can use our energies in productive ways rather than avoiding the troll. The question is this: Do we use our psychological energies to protect, defend, and stubbornly maintain our false self, or do we use those energies to explore, understand, and improve ourselves? Is our posture primarily open or antagonistic? The troll makes tremendous demands on us. He wants to be covered, defended, and shielded. He wants to be left under the bridge. When we refuse to explore him, his resistance functions like a virus. Fear of exposure has once again shut the door on self-discovery.

One of the best indicators of the healthiness of any group is the amount of blame that occurs. Sharing pain from our past, grieving childhood losses, and discussing how family behavior impacted us are different than blaming. The point of all grief work is to live again. The point of blaming is to excuse ourselves from living. While we need to put our lives in context (the psychological goings-on of our families-of-origin), we do not need to blame that context for everything wrong with us now. Today we are not victims. At one point in our lives, we were. We were utterly dependent upon other people to shape our sense of acceptability. Understanding and discussing that period of intense vulnerability does not have to mean that we are still vulnerable. The more we understand about what happened to us, the more "response-able" we become. Alternative choices are available.

Judging, evaluating, assessing, and analyzing others functions as a drug for many of us. It becomes the "fix" we need to escape our inner lives. By obsessing on the depravity of others, we distract our attention, gain a euphoric "buzz" of superiority, and experience an adrenalin rush from policing someone else's behavior. Gossiping and criticizing become more and more necessary as we continue to avoid self-reflection. Once again, the simple rule is this: When we're judging others, we're avoiding ourselves. We can forget about what **we** need to change, how **we** are lacking, and how **we** contribute to problems. Our accusations against others temporarily release us. We alter our moods by dissecting and ridiculing them. Deep within, our ongoing suspicion of inadequacy must be relieved through blaming someone. The painful reality is this: No amount of external judgment will heal our internal need for grace.

Judgment of others is most often a form of self-disgust. Others "pick up the tab" for our refusal to embrace, accept, and become familiar with our own trolls. The battle within gets pushed outward. The enemy becomes projected so that we can crusade against what we secretly hate in ourselves. Others are manipulated into scapegoat carriers of our own shame. We rail against them, denounce them, and proudly wonder how they became so vile. They are the targets of our own self-contempt.

Many television evangelists are painfully troll-based. They illustrate this point that judgment is born out of self-disgust. Pounding pulpits, pointing fingers, and spitting out prophetic pronouncements, they angrily gloat that they are the "conscience of America" or the "true voice of God." As we listen to their soapbox fanaticism and "God-endorsed" rage, we begin to realize that they are really dealing with their own trolls. Prejudice, displaced anger, repressed sexuality, authoritarian thinking, ethnocentrism, interpersonal rigidity, internal conflict, and tons of self-disgust are proclaimed as the "word of God." Enormous pretense and arrogance hides behind their claim to "own" divine truth.

When the troll's aggressive attacks are given religious sanction as "God's wrath," the problem of self-disgust is compounded. Religion is then used to camouflage self-hate. Frustrated and riddled with inner tension, many preachers externalize their dilemma and do battle with a multitude of sinful enemies. They seem, of necessity, to perpetually fight "something." Their graceless void within pushes them toward outside distractions. Judging becomes an all-consuming passion, an addiction, a sad necessity for self-avoidance. They become troll-bound.

Our judgments and criticism of others are usually based on our insecure need to prove our superiority. We must dominate and conquer. We must convert the enemy into something familiar. Fear governs our lives, but we cover this fear with aggression. The truth is that we are threatened. We don't know how to handle differences. Our insecurities push us into an attack.

It takes a secure individual to follow through with a "live and let live" philosophy. When **we** accept and like who we are, we are far more likely to let others be who **they** are. Do differences threaten us? If so, why? Again, it is because we are uncomfortable with who **we** are, not who someone else is. The discomfort is within. Any need to prove our superiority grows out of this self-doubt. To whom must we prove ourselves? The painful answer: to ourselves! We battle to demonstrate our adequacy. The disheartening fact is this: Because there are so many differences in the world, we will remain threatened. It will become a perpetual condition. Recoiled and defensive, we will not enjoy the varieties of people in the world. We'll be scared, so we'll have to act tough. What we lack in self-esteem we'll make up for in judgments.

This negativity can grow into sarcasm, cynicism, and hopelessness. "That won't work." "What a stupid idea!" "This project won't get off the ground." "I don't think that place would be fun on a vacation." "Why should I go out with him/her?" "I wouldn't want to work there." "That school is too far from home!" "I just don't think they like me." These comments serve a very important function. They keep attention away from the speaker's self-doubts by putting down something on the outside. Our own fears generate most of our negativity. Yet if we can condemn an activity, person, or place, we won't have to look at these fears and doubts lurking behind the put-downs.

This simple strategy of condemning an activity because we feel insecure about it can be illustrated in a sixth grade experience I remember. At a birthday party, a group of young girls decided they wanted to put on some music and dance. With whom were they going to dance? The guys. So, all of us not-so-secure guys huddled together and announced that dancing was "stupid." We were all tough athletes and did not want to participate in something so silly. The truth, of course, was that we were all afraid. But it was much easier for our trolls to put down the activity than to say that we were afraid to try.

Sadly, many of us go through our adult lives projecting our self-negativity and judgments onto anything new and unfamiliar. We denounce what we cannot easily master. As a result, we block growth and cheat ourselves out of a lot of fun.

Moving away from judgmentalism does not mean that we cease to have convictions. Nor does it mean that we stop making judgments. After all, being an ethical human being will obviously necessitate making judgments and decisions about life and human behavior. We have every right, for instance, to object to unfair, hurtful actions.

Judgmentalism, on the other hand, wants to go beyond a description of behavior. It is hungry to attack and shame the person behind the actions. Judgmentalism rushes toward a verdict of the person, not the deed.

It's very helpful to begin monitoring our blaming and judging patterns. Just notice them. We need not berate ourselves because of them. Then we'll have two problems: our judging habits and our judgmentalism **about** those judging habits! Instead, we can more gently ask ourselves what we may be dodging or avoiding through our judgmental mentality. Again, the way out of judgment is compassion, not more judgment.

4.

Aloofness and Detachment: Being "Too Cool" for Our Troll

Life is often messy, unpredictable, uncertain, and ambiguous. It sometimes does not fit our desire for neat categories, clear-cut order, precision, and consistency. We often become anxious when we stop long enough to consider that in spite of our best efforts to build security, nothing is guaranteed. The unexpected, the tragic, the random element could be hurled into our path at any moment. The future dangles in the darkness of a big question mark. What will happen? How is our health? How secure are our relationships? Will our job persist? Will we find a job? How long will our families be with us? How strong is our faith? Is depression around the next corner? Will we regret moving? Will we regret staying? How do we know anything for sure? Are we spinning our wheels? Does anything ultimately matter?

The anxiety triggered by these questions is both the burden and the blessing of being human. The troll wants to beat us up when we do not have easy answers to these difficult concerns. At times these issues are a frightening annoyance. Sometimes we do not want to be bothered by them. At other times, the mysteries of life excite us, puzzle us, and invite us into our depths. But those depths can be frightening, bewildering, and threatening. We may be tempted to immediately withdraw and go back to where it feels safe. In one of his sermons, Paul Tillich puts this very well.

It is comfortable to live on the surface so long as it remains unshaken. It is painful to break away from it and to descend into an unknown ground. The tremendous amount of resistance against that act in every human being and the many pretexts invented to avoid the road into the depth are natural. The pain of looking into one's own depth is too intense for most people. They would rather return to the shaken and devastated surface of their former lives and thoughts...But the mark of real depth is its simplicity. If you should say, "This is too profound for me; I cannot grasp it," you are self-deceptive. For you ought to know that nothing of real importance is too

32

profound for anyone. It is not because it is too profound, but rather because it is too uncomfortable, that you shy away from the truth.[3]

As we refuse to face the insecurities inherent in life, we build walls of rigid, controlled thinking. We insist that life conform to our pre-arranged plan. The troll hates ambiguity because it interferes with his simplistic judgments. When he bumps into anything that seems unusual or different, he labels that thing and shuffles it into a familiar category. All things must match his simplistic categories. He is a "mystery buster." He abhors the unfamiliar and detests anything that cannot be quickly "put in its place." The world must be kept orderly and tidy at any cost! Life is thus something to be managed rather than experienced and embraced. It is a "thing" that must be subjected to our control. Life must be tamed, organized, and domesticated. Uncertainties must be squeezed out.

This excessive control is particularly seen in the world of human emotion. In fact, one of the most annoying aspects of life for a cool calculator is the complex world of feelings. It takes a great deal of work to turn our jungle of emotions into a fastidious terrain. Feelings cannot always be "figured out." It may be impossible to track down their roots. There are limits to what we can analyze. Nevertheless, aloof controllers believe all feelings must be accounted for, reasonable, and, above all else, never exaggerated. Being a grown-up, mature, and stable person is equated with not being very emotional. After all, powerful feelings threaten a strong, "together" image. Feelings get in the way of a business-as-usual life. All emotions must answer to the troll. And the troll has small parameters on the feelings he will allow.

Irene's False Sense of Security

Consider Irene. Irene had been a very shrewd and calculating business woman who believed emotions only get people in trouble. She had trained herself to live above her feelings. She reflected a calm, sophisticated reserve that let others know she was in control. Avoiding her inner life became second nature to her. She had a way of bringing all conversation around to the "bottom line." And the bottom line, for Irene, was always material and financial. Her aloofness became a defense against getting to

know herself or anyone else very well. She measured people according to their materialistic status and spartan-like invulnerability to emotion. Strong feelings, about anything, represented a refusal to grow up. She was a realist, a take-charge person, a controller. She didn't have time for the sidetracking and bewildering world of emotion. And she had no idea that she was scared to death of her own troll.

Irene's detached, aloof disposition came out clearly in her relationship with her sisters. One sister, Ann, was particularly emotional and easily provoked to tears. Whether it was the soft-hearted identification with a suffering person or feeling her own woundedness, Ann did not hold back her sadness when she felt it. Irene would immediately assume a condescending posture toward Ann's "childish feelings." She saw these emotions as weak and a source of embarrassment. Irene's injunctions to Ann always emphasized being strong and acting grown up. By ridiculing and shaming Ann's natural feelings, Irene communicated that appearance is everything.

Irene did very well in business. Because she and her husband devoted their lives to the sacred accumulation of wealth, all their energies were poured into this singular pursuit. They did not take time to feel much of anything. Their world of dinner parties, extravagant boats and cars, glittering clothes, and financial wizardry spoke for them. They had no idea how to respond to a psychological or spiritual question about their inner lives. They would immediately pull it to the surface—and the surface was about material and financial matters.

Irene became more and more of a calculating iceberg. Even her three children were evaluated on the basis of appearance, performance, and social maturity. "Don't let people know what you're feeling, because then they might use it against you." This seemed to be the numbed-out instruction from mother to child.

Irene displayed her control-sickness the most clearly when her mother died. Devastated by the untimely demise of their mom, two of the daughters were deeply sorrowed and disoriented. Irene, who would never allow herself beneath the surface of her feelings, began an obsessive fixation on what her mother owned. Assessing her mother's worth, and making sure that her mother's insurance money and other valuables were under her control, became a rather disgusting preoccupation. She justified her actions by saying that her other two sisters were too weak or too emotional to take care of business. Yet "taking care of business" was just another attempt to feed her craving for more. Security was in accumulated wealth. Because she was not burdened by the world of strong feelings, Irene was able to financially strategize during her own mother's funeral. She could not turn off her calculating, money-making schemes, even when it meant cheating her siblings out of their inheritance.

It may not look like it on the surface, but Irene's life is permeated with shame. Her troll is constantly at work, and she is taking the wrong medicine for her illness. Ashamed of her family background and maiden name, she attempts to rewrite her history through pretense. Yet no amount of money, prestige, or calculating control can completely shut the troll up. Her deep-rooted suspicion of inadequacy, in spite of her attempts to silence it, compulsively drives her.

The only effective way for Irene to deal with her anxiety is to hug it, claim it, experience it, and quit fighting it. There is no fortress that will keep her safe from the precarious events of life. She may try to eliminate her emotional needs, but they will return in distorted, ugly forms. Like any addict, her focus has narrowed. She has developed a materialistic tunnel vision. Life **is** money. By obsessing on this false form of security, and perpetuating an aloof image, Irene has eliminated close relationships with her sisters and with her children. And perhaps saddest of all, she has run away from herself. Irene has traded in the richness of life for a few illusory moments of control. Material answers do not heal spiritual questions.

Moving Beyond Our False Securities

The sad irony is that the very elements we are trying to "kill" (emotion, mystery, ambivalence, paradox, uncertainty, wonder) are the elements that feed vitality, energy, creativity, and meaning. Without them, the world becomes ordinary, mundane, stagnant, and insufferably predictable. Life loses its awe. It is hard to have amazement without having a-maze-ment. The price so often paid for manageable feelings is a lack of flair and enthusiasm.

Put directly, the issue is this: When we run away from our depths, we also run away from our resurrections. When we run away from our trolls, we run away from our healing. The solid, stable, ordinary world must crack and open to what pulsates below it. If we cannot die to our various false securities, we cannot know the real strengths buried within us. By hiding our weakness, we hide our strength. Without a crossroads, a crisis, or a struggle, the human spirit simply does not break through the troll's limits and find renewal. Hopelessness is part of the journey to hope. The collapse of certainty is a forerunner of faith.

5.

Anger, the Troll, and Healthy Conflict

Conflict can be frightening, challenging, bewildering, a waste of time, or a chance to bully someone. It can be a vehicle of growth or a debilitating hassle. It can lead to justice or it can promote injustice. It can be used in the service of deepening our humanity or it can be a dehumanizing instrument. We can exploit it, avoid it, or approach it with humility and a desire for fairness. Conflict can offer us an opportunity for deep self-awareness. Conflict explores, like no other interpersonal activity, what we think and feel about ourselves. It pulls back the curtain of self-esteem and shows us many assumptions about our being. In short, it exposes our troll.

Our past experience with conflict may have been so damaging that we see little, if any, use in it at all. Perhaps we watched conflict lead to verbal insults, explosive screaming, or people getting hit. Irreparably hurt feelings may have prevented, for years, people from talking with one another. If we saw nothing good come from conflict, we may have condemned the emotion of anger. What's the value of it? It only gets people into trouble.

It's easy to confuse anger (the feeling) with angry behavior. We may think anger means slapping someone, calling a person obscene names, or leaving a relationship. In fact, this may be the way we define anger. When threatened, the troll can do ugly things in the name of anger. Yet these are all behaviors about anger, and not anger itself. Anger is simply a human energy with which many things (not just violent ones) can be done. Because it is such potent energy, anger must be attended to with respect. This fiery feeling can be the tool of justice as well as the fuel of violence. When we condemn the emotion of anger because we don't express it constructively, we throw the baby out with the bath water.

It's important to look at our own gut-level assumptions about anger, because these assumptions regulate much of our behavior. We may tell people that anger is a natural, normal emotion. But what do we feel in our stomach about anger? What have been our "gut-learnings" about it? For instance, I remember teaching classes on anger-management in which I stated unequivocally that anger is a neutral, human, inevitable feeling. I went on to say that we need this emotion if we are to be fully

37

human. Yet in the privacy of my own feelings, I was phobic about anger. I wanted to dodge conflict. I often tried to resolve everyone else's anger because I was uncomfortable with it. I was an anger-dodger the whole time I spoke about the importance of accepting anger. My "appropriate" comments about the okay-ness of anger were a mere cerebral exercise that did not register in my gut.

It's only when we are in the face of conflict that we can truly access our deepest beliefs about conflict. As hard as it may be, if we can stay with the process, we can learn much about ourselves. Let's look at some of the most common patterns of handling anger, and what those patterns say about our troll.

Anger Pattern No. 1—Troll-Denial

With this approach, we assume that conflict never accomplishes anything. We might lose control. Or worse, someone might abandon us. So, we become afraid to be direct. Being straightforward always seems cold, and we cannot stand to hurt anyone's feelings. So we eat our anger, deny our irritations, and sweep our frustrations under a rug of repression. We don't want to be rejected. We can't say "no." In fact, we're easily manipulated because of this fear of rejection. We take a passive and superficial stance toward conflict. Harmony at all costs—that's our unconscious motto. We often confuse "being dependable" with being used. The troll turns us into a stranger to our own rights, feelings, and desires. Our own needs have been neglected for so long that we don't even know they're present. The troll says we don't have the permission to become angry. Security is more important than truth. We don't trust ourselves and we don't trust others, at least not enough to be honest. Phoniness is the price we pay for safety.

This approach to conflict is born out of low self-esteem, and keeps us chained to the troll's commentary about us. We don't have the right to speak up for ourselves, much less become angry. Anger is tied to self-protection, and if we have no right to protect ourselves, anger is out of the question. We become a doormat and non-assertive victim. We don't develop a defense for our own uniqueness. We give ourselves away to the most aggressive bidder. Our own troll runs over us so often that we let everyone else run over us too. This process obviously contributes to a decreasing self-respect. At some level, we know we are not protecting our own uniqueness. Put simply, without anger available, we cannot value ourselves.

Anger Pattern No. 2—Troll-Explosion

In this approach, we often let people "drive us crazy." We fly off the handle at all their foul-ups. And those people had better listen to us! After all, if we want to get ahead in life, we've got to push some people around. Our suspicions of inadequacy have set us up with a chip on our shoulder. The troll is turned outward. People must know where we stand. Sometimes we may lack impulse-control. Sometimes we may come across as insensitive, controlling, reactionary, blaming, and critical. Others may think we don't hear their viewpoint. Nonsense! We hear people when they've got something to say. The point is that we've got to be decisive, and that means not making mistakes. When we let people know we're vulnerable, we're asking for trouble. If a difference arises with others, they are simply wrong. It's never our fault. We know what we're doing. Our reality is the only reality. If we haven't experienced it, it's not real. Admitting uncertainties and insecurities always has a domino effect. Others are wrong and it's our job to point it out to them.

Low self-esteem clearly dangles from this approach. It may not look like it, but a fear of inadequacy pushes us toward aggression and a refusal to genuinely hear others. We are simply afraid. We are saying to other people, "I can't deal with my troll, so you try to handle him." Our fear moves us toward interpersonal violence. What is hard for us to see is that interpersonal hostility grows out of internal rioting against ourselves. We're constantly afraid of our opinion of ourselves, so we engage in constant compensations. If we can dominate, get the upper hand and conquer, then we can temporarily turn off the negative voices.

Again, we troll-explosive people often think we are responding to outside stress. The truth, however, is that we are normally reacting to inside stress. We are struggling with the critical messages, exaggerated interpretations, and self-doubts of the troll inside us. We are on edge, ready to believe the worst about life. The inner warfare is pushed outward. We don't really like ourselves, and the rest of the world has to pay for this self-disgust.

Anger Pattern No. 3—Unexpected Exploder

This approach is a combination of the first two. Most of the time we're nice, passive and easy-going. We will walk an extra mile to avoid a conflict. We hate to fight. We associate anger with violence, so we avoid it. We are nice people without trolls. We push our anger underground and store it in our bodies. We take and take from people, then we finally explode. This may not happen very often, but when it does, it is quite ugly. We feel overloaded and end up letting some innocent person "have it." It's as if we've been storing dynamite in the basement and someone strikes a match in the wrong spot. After we explode, we feel immediate guilt, start apologizing, then go on a campaign to make it up to that person. We swear that it won't happen to us again, but we can't seem to control it. We're like a walking time bomb. We move from "no anger" to the troll's rage, with nothing in-between.

This method of handling anger forgets the power of resentments. If we do not express anger while it is manageable, it will snowball into something we cannot handle constructively. Once again, this approach assumes we don't have the right to express irritations, annoyances, and frustrations. We wait until these feelings have turned into outrage. In our excessive concern with appearing nice, we end up becoming the very person we do not want to be. We don't want to appear petty. We don't want to be perceived as "difficult." Out of insecurity and a need to appear as though we are something we're not, we tell ourselves we don't have a right to express our aggravations. Others may have this right, but we don't! We have a more-than-human image to uphold.

When we finally express our anger, it is quite impossible to handle it in a healthy manner. Our explosion contributes to low self-esteem, and furthers our belief that we have no business expressing anger. We tell ourselves that it is bad for us, and that it is one of the emotions we should leave alone. We ridicule and condemn ourselves for our last explosive "show." We're convinced that everyone is talking about how out-of-control we've become. Our shame becomes a set-up for more passivity. We'll start the same process again, and end up with another self-esteem-debilitating rage attack.

Healing will entail the uncomfortable experience of expressing our rights and feelings even when the issue seems small or petty. This will ensure a lack of accumulation. We have the right to speak up before the issue gets out of hand.

Anger Pattern No. 4—Quiet Revenge

This approach is also passive-aggressive, but it differs a bit from unexpected explosion. Here, we have the ultimate weapon—guilt. We don't get angry. We only get wounded and withdraw. People are always "hurting us," but we do not directly strike back. In fact, we may even do all sorts of nice things for these people. We might even give them gifts as we hope they will be ashamed of themselves for what they've said or done. We'll just continue being "nice" to them because they need to wallow in their guilt. We'll keep score. They owe us. There are strings attached to our acts of kindness. We use silence as a deadly punishment. We frequently display our pain and suffering as ways of maintaining control. We will drop hints, withdraw affection, or become a martyr in order to silently, but surely, get even!

This "under-the-table" approach to conflict respects neither our own anger nor anyone else's ability to hear it with fairness and understanding. Our anger is denied, then used as a manipulative tool. By not appreciating this anger as part of our genuine selfhood, we alienate it, then use it as a weapon. This further decreases our self-esteem because we know that we are not being honest. Our self-esteem always pays a heavy price when we are not real. By being dishonest, we encourage the suspicion that honesty would destroy us.

Suggestions for Healthy Conflict

Conflict often takes us to the heart of what we believe about ourselves. It exposes our assumptions. While it is certainly uncomfortable, conflict provides an opportunity for self-learning that is not otherwise available. But how can we accept ourselves in the middle of conflict? How can we deal with our anger in a constructive manner? How can we build, rather than tear down, our self-esteem in the middle of our clashes with people?

1. Be patient with old conflict patterns. Our first step in constructively handling conflict is to be patient with our patterns of handling anger. These patterns were not developed overnight, and they cannot be instantly changed. Perhaps we could look closely at what we saw modeled in our family-of-origin. How have those displays of anger influenced us? How many of those conflict patterns do we still carry? It is important to sort out our parents' conflict issues from our own. Maybe we have been psychologically carrying some of their anger, when it really does not belong to us. Separating our anger from their anger issues can be quite liberating.

Related to this, we can frequently talk about our anger with trusted friends. Please notice that I said "trusted" friends. Discussing what seems to trigger our anger, what patterns have not worked, what types of situations provoke us can be very helpful. This helps us feel more comfortable, and less panicky, about anger.

As we identify the kinds of people who push our buttons, perhaps we can explore whether this tells us something about our own dark side and unfinished business. In other words, as we react to others, are we really reacting to ourselves? Are we transferring the problem outward? We may well find that as we accept more of ourselves, we have less issues with others.

2. Simply notice the early stages of anger. It is crucial to simply notice our anger. Don't shame it, judge it, or frantically try to get rid of it. It's just there. Often, our prohibition against anger causes us far more problems than the anger itself. The anger is seeking our attention. Perhaps we can choose to attend to it. As a feeling passing through our bodies, it has something to say. We need not shut it out or ignore it.

Many times, shamed anger comes back around as rage. Because it has been prohibited or ignored, it seeks our attention with a much louder voice. "This time," it says, "by God, you will pay attention." Rage is normally historical anger, ignored anger, and anger with a "chip on its shoulder." It has accumulated a lot of energy.

It's important, then, to recognize anger states at their beginnings. We can detect irritations, annoyances, and frustrations before they snowball into outrages. Anger, in its early stages, often flees our awareness like a frightened animal. We think it's "silly" or "immature" to feel angry, so we tell ourselves it's not really anger. But as we chase our anger away, we are inviting it to woundedly withdraw, accumulate more strength, then come back when it is too large to handle. By ignoring our anger, we are setting ourselves up to be hurt by it.

3. Own the anger as *our* feeling, and, hence, *our* problem. We can recognize anger as our feeling and realize that it does little good to blame others for making us mad. Other people's behavior may be intricately involved in our anger, but it is still our anger, and we are left with the problem of what to do with it.

42

We also need to remember that if we don't feel comfortable with our own anger, then we probably won't feel comfortable with anyone else's, either. We may downplay or minimize it because we're disturbed by it. We may unconsciously communicate to others that anger is off limits. We're too "nice" for it. We couldn't handle it. Anger-phobic people can manipulate others by inviting a phony pleasantness.

4. Make a quick over-reaction inventory. Without denying what we feel, we can ask ourselves if we are overreacting to a situation. Are we interpreting an event in all-or-nothing, exaggerated ways, and thereby inflaming our anger? Are we blowing things out of proportion? Are we making more of something that we need to? If we are, we can once again simply notice what this may be telling us about our own fears and insecurities.

Much of our overreaction results from twisting a desire into a demand. Are we turning a preference into an absolute need? Are we insisting that life conform to what we hope it will be? We often set ourselves up for unnecessary anger with our own demands. It's easy to develop a private set of rules about the way other people and life itself **should** be. When these rules do not match reality, we then become infuriated. But the anger-producing mechanism is in our own expectations. The world must conform to what we want. It's important to gently back out of some of these demands and accept life on life's terms. This does not mean that we passively receive, in a victim's position, whatever comes to us. We can most definitely work toward justice, change unfairness in the world, and leave the planet a little more humane than we found it. Yet we won't have the energy to change what we can if we're constantly frustrated by trying to change what we cannot. Recalling the serenity prayer can do wonderful things for our anger-management. When we try to control the uncontrollable, we rob ourselves of life-affirming energy. Our anger must be a constructive energy if we are to change injustice.

5. Recognize the need for a time-out. Another factor in constructively handling our anger is realizing when we may need a time-out to calm down. This is not an admission of weakness. This is simply recognizing that we all have a point in which anger can no longer be expressed in a healthy way. We need a break, a cool-down period. Postponing a confrontation does not necessarily involve anger-denial. In fact, it may be because we are acutely aware of our anger that we know we need this time-out. Deferring our anger can be a sign of strength rather than an indication of weakness.

6. Avoid the troll's tendency toward verbal violence. If we want anger to lead us toward justice and interpersonal peace, we need to avoid name-calling, trigger words, labeling, and other forms of verbal violence. It will be exceedingly tempting to blast someone with a colorful, descriptive expletive in the middle of an anger spiral. Yet the temporary rush we experience from doing this is not worth the interpersonal damage done. Further, our own self-esteem is negatively affected when we allow someone else the power to decompose our calm status. We can say what we need to say without becoming violent.

The problem, however, is that many of us are accustomed to violence. The troll has been talking this way to **us** for years. So, the place to begin cleaning up these violent attacks is at home. When we refuse to rage against, ridicule, or harshly condemn ourselves, this becomes excellent practice for when we deal with others. We can start by making a pact with ourselves. A helpful question is this: Have we ever changed, been motivated, or altered a significant behavior because of the troll's labeling or screaming at us? Raging against ourselves only sets us up for a rebellion, further warfare, and a greater split inside. Since the antagonistic method has not worked, why not at least try a more gentle approach? What do we have to lose? The other way is not working anyway.

Another form of interpersonal violence involves dredging up historical issues, then slinging mud at the person because of the past. We open old wounds, and protest once again our objections to this past hurt. Today's anger quickly jumps into yesterday's issues. Old pain is marched before the person with a bitter accusation, "Look what you've done."

This pattern of punishing someone with the past is often hard to turn off. Certainly we need to allow ourselves to grieve this wound. And when we stay in the backwaters of resentment, we have not really expressed how we have been hurt. Anger feels safer than hurt so we stay there. "How could you have done this to me?" is a safer question than "How have I been hurt by this?" While hurt and anger are normally two sides of the same coin, it is often easier, and less painful, to stay on the anger side. On this side, we can focus on the other person's behavior, rather than on how we feel. When we don't express our hurts directly, they later come out twisted. These twisted hurts get recycled over and over because they are not directly expressed. Again, it's much easier to talk about how awful **they** are than how devastated **we** feel. So, mud-slinging often indicates that our deepest layer of hurt has not really been heard.

Also, forgiving and embracing our own past can go a long way in helping us accept someone else's past. As we become more caringly attentive to ourselves, less judgmental, and more aware that our past choices were not deliberately malicious, perhaps we can extend some of this grace outward to others. If we quit throwing our past up to **ourselves**, perhaps we will quit throwing other people's past up to **them**.

Related to this interpersonal problem, we need to avoid generalizations. "You're always late." "You're just lazy." "You're stupid." "You're totally irresponsible." Words such as never, always, absolutely, completely, and totally are not words that lead to interpersonal peace. The other person feels condemned, not instructed. There is no information within these judgments, only condemnations.

Finding Balance

Sometimes it is liberating to remember that we don't **have** to work things out with everyone with whom we have conflict. Sometimes a healthy resolution is just not possible. It's important to take care of ourselves in this process. This may mean minimizing, or in some cases eliminating, contact with people who are toxic for us. This does not necessarily indicate cowardice; instead, it may demonstrate self-care. People will sometimes try to control, invade, or dominate us. We need not be shocked when this happens. This is simply the way life is.

Neither, however, do we need to become paranoid about people invading our boundaries. Our anger can shield and protect us. Unhealthy guilt and low self-esteem will tell us that we do not have the right to our boundaries. Yet our anger, especially when we detect it early, tells us that we are worthy of self-protection. Without anger, we are prey.

The discomfort felt when we first start to become assertive is certainly worth it. Again, it will often feel unnatural. That's okay. All new behavior feels uncomfortable at first. We may have to act with confidence before we feel confident. Strength and security often follow, rather than precede, action.

If our conflict problems are often a symptom of a self-problem, then what can we do about it? If we want to change, how do we get started? How do we "go to work" on ourselves? Perhaps the way we have approached "changing" has created more problems than solutions. Maybe we have turned ourselves into another object we have tried to manipulate into "growth." It's possible that in our highly intentional, rigor-

45

ous, no-nonsense method of fixing ourselves, we have made little progress. Perhaps, instead, we have accumulated a great deal of frustration.

Let's turn our attention toward a different approach to change. Perhaps our distraught attempt to "get" self-esteem has resulted from an over-focused preoccupation with ourselves. Let's look at the possibility that developing self-esteem is somewhat paradoxical. Maybe self-acceptance results from relaxing with who we are rather than chasing who we need to become.

6.

Accepting Our Troll
(A Healing Paradox)

Many of us desperately want self-esteem. We attend workshops. We read scores of self-help books. We weave in and out of therapy. We may be active in twelve-step groups, church groups, singles groups, couples groups, and other community functions. We are relentlessly focused on "getting" more self-esteem and accumulating more positive feelings about ourselves. Self-esteem, we believe, is a state of being we are trying to track down. We'll trap and internalize it.

Often, we expect magic. An immediate, life-changing, never-to-be-doubted experience is sought. We await the dramatic arrival of self-esteem. At 3:10 p.m. on a Thursday afternoon in our therapist's office, the right insight will usher in this new reality! Or, on a rainy Saturday evening, while we devour the third self-help book we've looked at this week, a wave of angelic confidence will change forever that nagging self-doubt floating around in our belly (the troll). All will be different when we "get it." Now, of course, we don't have it. But there are new books to read, new seminars to attend, and new avenues to "the answer." Unfortunately, many of these hopes for tomorrow cancel out today's importance.

The frantic search for inward wealth can be as compulsive as an outward search for material wealth. Our own growth can become an obsessive, exclusive preoccupation. Self-analysis can degenerate into an addictive habit. Ironically, the constant worry about how to live better can itself be an avoidance of life. By the time we have figured it out, life is over. In the meantime, how do we live? Many have pointed out the problem of becoming addicted to physical exercise. But what about the problem of being addicted to "inward" exercise?

I remember once participating in a conversation with people in a twelve-step program in which the whole idea of "growth" began to sound like cross-addiction. We discussed the dangers of obsessing on alcohol, cocaine, food, sex, unhealthy relationships, and so on. Then, however, it became progressively obvious that we were "obsessed on discussing obsessions." Identifying addictions had itself become an addiction. Personal awareness had evolved into a compulsive, legalistic, joyless habit. "Growth" itself had become our new drug of choice. Self-transcendence was lacking. An excruciating seriousness dominated our jargon. Further, the world was basically divided into two camps: those who were in "the program" (psychological self-help or twelve-step groups), and those who were not. If others did not know our particular recipe for personal change and growth, they had probably found no spiritual foundation elsewhere. Our group went on to talk about the rigidity in much of institutional religion. While many of our assessments of authoritarian religion were probably accurate, we needed a challenge to look at our own brand of narrowly-focused spirituality.

The point here is certainly not to knock "growth language" or rigorous discussions about the good life. In fact, that kind of criticism would go against the grain of this book. Yet what seems to create problems for many of us is a mania about personal improvement. Measuring our lives on the basis of how many meetings we attend each week, spending our vacation time going to yet another convention or workshop, turning the most interesting conversations into opportunities to soapbox about our particular string of dysfunctions, and constantly using code language (recover-ese) may well indicate that we are over the edge. The recovery movement is for living, not the other way around. For many of us, talking about living can easily become a substitute for the real thing.

Sometimes it is helpful to remind ourselves that we will die with great uncertainty about who we really are. Our inner world is often like the mysterious depths of the ocean. We just don't know what's there. The task then becomes accepting and appreciating ourselves right square in the middle of this ignorance. This does not provoke us to resign our research, but it does give our agenda a more modest, and human, quality. Again and again, after tasting a genuine insight into who we are, we return to a mystery. So much within us will remain, of necessity, uncharted.

Getting in Our Own Way

Consider, for a moment, a runner who does quite well until he starts to study his feet. Imagine a speaker who hypnotically holds our attention until she starts worrying about how she is coming across. Visualize an insomniac trying desperately to fall asleep. Envision a child trying **not** to notice something.

In all of these examples, we get in our own way. By narrowing our focus and getting preoccupied with ourselves, we actually distract from what we are doing. Our zealous intentionality can turn into a self-sabotaging device. By trying too hard, or becoming fixated on what we are attempting, we reduce our chances of doing it. Sex therapists, for instance, tell us much about the performance-anxiety that so many men feel when they demand of themselves that "tonight has to be the night." When these men allow themselves to relax and lay down their demands and expectations, spontaneously natural things can happen. But as long as they are agitatedly trying to make things happen, their control often backfires.

Suppose we are going to get together with a friend and talk. Ordinarily, we find this person extremely easy to confide in. But let's say that at this particular meeting, we announce that we will now have a "stimulating conversation." We sit and stare at each other, not knowing what to say. It doesn't seem the same. In fact, it seems unnatural and contrived. What would have happened automatically is now blocked because of our announcement.

So what's the point here? Simply that our own well-intentioned, but compulsive, efforts can block, rather than promote, our development. When we try too hard to have fun, be romantic, like someone, or not be self-conscious, the result is almost always the same: self-defeating. Our anxieties push our control buttons. Instead of allowing things to happen, we try to make them happen.

The Problem with Troll-Killing

Our desperate and obsessive attempts to change are especially troublesome in dealing with our troll. When we "try too hard" to fix our self-esteem problems, we make some self-defeating assumptions. These assumptions are often quite violent. We approach part of ourselves as the enemy who must be destroyed. The reasonable, self-affirming, relationship-skilled part of us must track down some hideous inward distortion and eliminate this "thing." The troll must be thrown away. The reasonable, positive side of us must perform a search-and-destroy mission. Our immaturities must be smoked out, our irrationalities attacked, our depression combatted, and our inferiority fought. In short, we must take charge by invading, conquering, and dominating our troll. The goal is demolition, not integration.

There are some significant beliefs tied to this philosophy of troll-killing. Some of these beliefs include the following:

1. Something is desperately wrong with us.
2. We need to kill, rip out, or completely change our troll in some crucial way.
3. Self-esteem is "something" we don't have.
4. "Getting" self-esteem will necessitate murdering our troll.
5. Other people look and sound more "together" than we **feel**, so they must not be bothered by the troll.
6. If we keep doing battle, we will someday have self- esteem.

These assumptions, as part of the whole troll-killing framework, are based on a rather violent image of change. We end up fragmented and split up inside. Part of us plays the role of the authoritarian parent and dictator who is going to whip the troll into line or get rid of him altogether. We will forcibly make ourselves change! More willpower—that's the secret for getting rid of our troll.

The problem, however, is that this sort of relationship with ourselves involves the worst form of autocratic parenting. A superior, condescending, arrogant part of us looks down upon and criticizes the undisciplined part (our troll). In the meantime, we completely forget that the word discipline comes from the word disciple. Disciples follow something they love. Following something we love is quite different from bowing down to an authoritarian tyrant.

This troll-killing approach sets us up for a civil war underneath our own skin. Just as teenagers frequently revolt against authoritarian, rigid parents, so we as individuals rebel against our own internal demands. The troll loves to fight anyway. Insisting that we get rid of him fuels his resistance and creates inner tension. We can easily spot this in a family system. But the same process occurs in our own awareness.

Thus, we set ourselves up for an "internal battle of Gettysburg." The troll remains squatting in the shadows under the bridge. He actually wants to be loved and accepted into the daylight, but he won't admit it. It's simply not helpful to use shame on the troll. He won't budge that way. Besides, that's his game. When we divide ourselves this way, the troll develops resentments against his internal judge. The inner-sinner refuses to bow to the inner-Pharisee. We perpetuate our own troll's revolt, rebellion, and alienation because of this antagonism. One part of us simply won't accept the troll. The war continues as long as we play by the troll-killing rules.

If the shoot-out-at-noon game does not work with our nonconforming, trouble-making troll, then what do we do? Directly challenging and eliminating him is not effective. His resistance is too strong. What now?

The Most Difficult Admission—"We Are Our Troll"

The biggest problem with slaying our trolls is that we would be killing part of **ourselves!** That's right. As painful as it may be to admit, the troll is part of us. He's not some alien being who decided to contaminate our path, or some external reality imposing on us. The troll is part of our very being. His voice is our voice. His self-destruction is our death wish. His catty, critical, hyperjudgmental disposition toward life is part of our attitude.

This makes it even more imperative to avoid violence. The troll always wins at violence because he enjoys it. He has no qualms about doing whatever it takes to stop us from crossing a bridge. We simply do not want to do battle with him on his terms.

In spite of ugly threats, growls, and malicious tricks, the troll is afraid. He does not know how to handle it when we approach him out of care, compassion, and openness. He has felt rejected, cynical, and marooned under a bridge. He's angry because he's been hurt. That's understandable. The troll has no idea what to do with kindness. If he is embraced as part of the family, and we refuse to react to his muttering but instead see him as a lost part of ourselves who needs to be accepted, even the troll can become misty-eyed. He won't admit it, of course. But he knows that we know.

Dr. Jekyll and Mr. Hyde—An Excellent Troll Story

One of the most colorful and brilliant descriptions of an internal split with the troll is Robert Louis Stevenson's classic, **Dr. Jekyll and Mr. Hyde.**[4] When Stevenson wrote his Gothic tale in 1886, he had little idea his dichotomized creature would have such influence. Written before the impact of Freud's ideas about personality, Stevenson poetically describes the housing of contradictory selves within the same flesh, two forces warring for the governing control of the psyche. Because Stevenson's tale is such a potent example of the inward division with the troll, it seems worthy of our review.

If you remember the story, Henry Jekyll was a highly respected physician with a strong desire to separate his noble aspirations from his darker side. He wanted a life "above" or "beyond" his troll. To accomplish this, he created a troll-killing, chemical potion. He drank the concoction with great eagerness, thinking he had found the solution to his inner tensions. Much to his shock, Mr. Hyde, a sensual, selfish, aggressive madman emerged on the other side of the potion. Mr. Hyde is a marvelous example of the disowned troll. He is the exiled, ridiculed, rejected part of Henry Jekyll. Mr. Hyde did not fit into the image Jekyll wanted to portray, so Hyde was pushed underground. Recognition and acceptance might have redeemed the shadowy creature, but Jekyll refused to embrace Hyde. Ironically, by rejecting Hyde, Jekyll actually helped the grotesque creature grow stronger. The cure for the Hyde problem would have been ownership and acceptance of the self.

Jekyll reflected all the restrictions of a self-righteous Victorian conscience. In reality, however, he was tired of chasing his perfectionism. He was quite vulnerable to the excitement and energy of Edward Hyde. Jekyll's own mundane rules set him up for an enchantment with his rejected "other" half. Mr. Hyde had no need for the phony display of Jekyll's hypocritical world. Restriction, pretense, and inhibition had kept him prisoner. He hated them.

What does Stevenson's tale have to do with us? Well, even if we have not shone the flashlight of our awareness over into our own dark corner, Mr. Hyde lurks there. And our own pretensions and lack of self-acceptance make him much worse than he has to be. Like every dimension of us, Mr. Hyde wants to be recognized for what he is. When "accepted into the family," Mr. Hyde is not so bad. He may be eccentric, a bit impulsive, sensual, and irreverent. But who among us wants a life completely void of these elements? Mr. Hyde has much energy we need. Keeping him chained to our unconscious only makes him mad. And he will be recognized. He'll see to that.

Henry Jekyll died from a lack of self-acceptance. Stevenson's tale concludes with Jekyll killing himself. Even at the very end, Dr. Jekyll would not really own Mr. Hyde. Hyde was a hideous creature quite separate from the good doctor. Yet Jekyll's dual existence could go no further. The division was too painful. The split could no longer be fueled by denial.

When we refuse to acknowledge the conflicting voices within, we cut off part of ourselves we deem unacceptable. The cut-off, dismembered, hated part of ourselves hates back. Unrecognized, it roams with growing hunger to control our lives. The more quarantined we make the troll, the more diabolical and less human he becomes. Exposure, recognition, and acceptance would offer the possibility of balance. The troll longs for attention, and if he cannot get it directly, he will act out in disturbed ways. When cut off, he develops a vicious tenacity.

We are often so afraid of acting on our impulses that we deny their existence. The Hyde (troll) within becomes the shamed, unacknowledged orphan. As the one alienated from the rest of the personality, Hyde will be the first to point out our phoniness. Mr. Hyde's energies will go toward dethroning the saints.

Extending Grace to Mr. Hyde

Suppose Mr. Hyde were approached with a gentle, caring attentiveness. What if we saw him as we might see a wounded animal? What if, psychologically speaking, we invited him to dinner? What if (God forbid!) we acknowledged him exactly as he is, and expressed a desire to build a relationship? What if we gradually encouraged him into the light, rather than chased him back into the darkness?

Perhaps this type of self-acceptance could begin a process of pulling the pieces together. The road toward integration involves looking squarely into the face of our fragmentation. When the Jekyll in us lays down our painful judgments, the Hyde in us is less prone to act out of defensiveness. When our Jekyll quits making tyrannical demands, our Hyde may feel less need to rebel. As we realize that Hyde is Jekyll and Jekyll is Hyde, genuine change can take place.

But this is not a gimmick to trick our troll into changing. Instead, it is a jolting awareness that our convenient black-and-white categories are an illusion. The "good" and "bad" within cannot be separated and divided so easily. In fact, our identity is the tension between these two. The separation has cost us dearly and we desperately need at-one-ment.

Jekyll attempted to deal with his inward division through a chemical solution. The fear of gently loving himself was too great. The courage required to embrace his own dark brother was too much. Instead, Jekyll sought an easier way. He had no idea of his shadow's hidden strength.

Mr. Hyde is a reminder that grace precedes self-revelation. In fact, grace makes self-knowledge possible. We cannot know ourselves without a gentle, kind hand and a commitment to non-violence. Otherwise, it's too frightening. Mr. Hyde will simply remain in the shadows. He needs the assurance **in advance** that we will stick with him "no matter what." Conditional acceptance is not acceptance. Our troll won't be willing to take the risk. Consequently, from his headquarters in the shadows, he will control our behavior. The fear of rejection will keep him in his woundedness. As Theodore Rubin puts it, "The solemn, deep promise to be gentle with ourselves must be invoked again and again, before and during any process of self-revelation."[5]

Steps Toward Troll-Acceptance

The following suggestions are based around the words, "Troll Acceptance." Let's look at this list, then develop each suggestion a little more thoroughly.

T reat our troll with gentle strength
R ecognize our detours around the troll
O wn our troll as part of ourself
L et the troll have the floor, but not the final word
L ead our troll back to his fears

A cknowledge that self-acceptance is a daily practice
C onnect with supportive, non-shaming people
C onfront our troll's exaggeration and hype
E xpress feelings of inadequacy with trusted friends
P ursue goals without making them "gods"
T ry new things, even when we lack confidence
A llow no abusive relationships
N ame our strengths and gifts in front of our troll
C onnect with a vision or purpose larger than ourself
E nd the war between ourself and our troll

Let's examine more closely these suggestions. Our first step will necessitate the promise of not threatening or ridiculing our troll. If we approach him critically or antagonistically, we will not get far. A non-judgmental posture should seek only to understand his fears, not necessarily control them. Again, we are not picking a fight with the troll. We just want to know him better.

Next, we've seen how the various methods of getting around the troll push us even deeper into feelings of inadequacy. These detours may provide temporary relief, but nothing more. We need to become as familiar as possible with our own self-avoidant strategies. When are we in an act? How did we tune out our inner restlessness? For many of us, going numb can be as natural as breathing. In fact, we've learned our defenses and detours **too well**. It's time to start noticing, with a compassionate alertness, what it is we're afraid of.

"Owning" is a good word to describe self-acceptance. It points toward the integrity of claiming all aspects of our being. It is part of self-loyalty, the tenacious habit of inviting more and more of ourselves to come out into the light. This recognizes that each of us has mixed, hidden, and conflicting dimensions to our identity. Genuine self-acceptance must always embrace the troll. If we haven't seen our troll, listened to his intimidating voice, or felt his icy presence underneath our bridge, we need not talk of being integrated, accepting, balanced, or self-respecting.

The troll, like an unruly child, will not rest until he's been given some attention. Yet listening to the troll does not mean being controlled by what he says. We need not bow down to him, cater to him, sink in fear before him, or put him in the driver's seat. He is simply part of our reaction to situations. He has **a** voice, not **the** voice. Just as we can remain calm when a child tells us about a nightmare, we can listen with concerned detachment to the troll.

We can gently ask the troll what he is afraid of. He will, at first, probably say, "nothin'," in a crude, rugged voice. But eventually he may provide us with specific horror scenes he wants to avoid. Sometimes he will be less specific. It's important to remember that, in a distorted and disturbed way, even the troll is trying to protect us. He wants to keep us safe from risk or the possibility of getting even more hurt. It is often helpful to do non-intellectual exercises with our troll, such as drawing pictures of him, writing him letters, letting him write nasty letters to us, and listening to him in a non-judgmental and non-reactionary manner.

Again, as we listen to the troll, we can lead him back to his fears. What is really "eating at" the troll? What is he protesting? We need to look for the insecurity beneath his aggression. Why does he stay under the bridge? The troll will get nervous when we talk about abandonment, loneliness, intimacy, or childhood woundedness. It's safer for him to stay mad. Perhaps we can gradually lead him out of his protesting and into his hurting. This is admittedly difficult. He'll curse, denounce us, and say things such as, "I don't believe in that psycho-mumbo-jumbo garbage." After all, it's far easier for the troll to say "Life stinks!" than to say "I was hurt by that." Yet, secretly, the troll wants to be released from his imprisoning hurts.

Small, specific steps are important in accepting the troll. Trying to overthrow his fears overnight is not very realistic. We can learn much in this regard from the fellowship of Alcoholics Anonymous. Most recovering people panic at the thought of **never** drinking again. However, when they slice off a day at a time, and think only in the parameters of a twenty-four hour segment, life is manageable. The flood gates stay closed today, and as A.A. members frequently say, "It's always today."

A great deal of troll anxiety may be connected to not fitting in or feeling abnormal. It's important to look at what we so easily accept as "normal." Often, a socially-sanctioned definition of what's normal pushes us toward feeling estranged from society. Yet we may desperately need to examine the underpinnings of our culture. Do our deepest values match the broad stream of our society? Does normal always mean ethical, caring, significant, compassionate, and just? Often not.

Sam Keen frequently uses an analogy with personal computers to describe the cultural impact upon us. He says that it's as if each of us comes into the world with hardware (our bodies). Yet the minute we arrive (or even before we arrive!), the culture is ready with software. Program disks are inserted telling us what it means to be a midwestern male born into a Republican family. Or the program may tell us what it means to be born female into a Democratic New England family. Family and cultural expectations and definitions for being a normal person are unconsciously programmed into us before we even know what is happening.

A big part of waking up spiritually is taking out these programs and examining what fits our own experience. Accepting a pre-packaged program as normal, without ever questioning or challenging how our own experiences, thoughts, feelings, and sense of self fit into it, is quite dangerous. No wonder we feel alienated, alone, and anxious. Someone else's definition as to who we are and what we mean has been elevated over our own journey. We don't have to be slaves to this cultural baggage. In fact, genuine liberation comes with our ability to choose what describes our lives and what does not.

The troll feeds off criticism and negativity from people around us. He knows that a cynical, judgmental attitude is like a virus entering our bodies. Out of fear, the troll uses other people's unfavorable comments about us as ammunition for self-attack. Other troll-based people provide our own trolls with bigger and better clubs for self-beatings.

This is why it's so crucial to surround ourselves, as much as we can, with non-toxic, healthy people. These associations will strengthen and build us. We can often be "accepted into accepting ourselves." In other words, as we risk being known, and find ourselves acceptable to others, it becomes more feasible to accept ourselves also. Our friends and associates are crucial in providing us with insulation against the troll's attacks.

We need not resist confronting the irrational, highly exaggerated, abusive nature of the troll's remarks. We can care about the troll while we firmly challenge his distorted thinking. The important thing is to remain calm, non-reactionary, and simply analyze what the troll is saying. It's important to re-frame the troll's images in less hostile ways. We can refuse to be violent. And we can accept the troll as we sure-footedly tell him that his ideas are far-fetched and we have no intention of buying them. The troll knows we can dismantle his irrationalities if we stay calm. He is counting on us to overreact. We don't have to play into his game.

Expressing our feelings of inadequacy with trusted friends is like pouring cold water on the troll's indictments. The troll wants us in isolation. His shaming messages are more easily internalized that way. When others share our vulnerability and affirm our struggles with hope and encouragement, the troll's job becomes much more difficult.

Another important factor for troll acceptance is not turning a value (limited good) into a "god" (something pivotal for our existence).[6] Pursuing a value is a worthwhile endeavor which brings disappointment when it's not achieved. Chasing a "god," however, has devastating consequences if we don't succeed. The troll triggers our anxiety by saying we must do this thing or we're worthless. He then provokes our depression if we are not successful. He says, "Now you've lost everything." This is why it's crucial to keep our goals in perspective. The minute we elevate them to something we can't live without, the troll starts torturing us with images of failure.

The troll also wants to convince us that we never have enough confidence to try new things. He suggests that confidence is a magical thing that must precede action. Once we get self-assurance, we can embark on a task, but not until then! The truth, of course, is that confidence comes as a result of taking a risk. It does not drop into our lap from out of nowhere. It is built with calculated risks and exercises of self-trust. If we wait on total confidence, we'll wait forever.

Another issue in making peace with our trolls is not allowing ourselves to stay involved in abusive relationships. Abusive relationships can do tremendous damage to our self-esteem. Why? Because it becomes two against one. The abusive person outside of us is teamed up with our inner abuser, the troll. The troll will take the abuse and use it against us in a couple of ways. First, he'll tell us we have no right to stand up for ourselves, so we should take it. Then second, after we've taken it, he'll ridicule us for getting run over again. We can't win. The troll always reinforces the abuser's attacks. Self-care necessitates putting a stop to both outward and inward violence.

Another important troll-accepting habit is to name our strengths in front of the troll. He will, of course, belittle, minimize, or even laugh at our strengths. However, when we insist upon acknowledging them, we greatly reduce the troll's debunking. In fact, he seems to develop a new kind of respect for us. We learn to cling to our gifts and talents no matter what the troll says. His voice is not reality, and we know it. His perspective is born out of fear and is highly distorted. The troll wants us to stay as miserable as he is.

We also need to remember that when we commit ourselves to a purpose, vision, or sense of "mission" that is our true passion, our self-esteem is greatly helped. Self-fulfillment is a fringe benefit of our heart's commitment to values, ideals, and a way of life we believe in. Chasing private, internal meanings without connecting those issues to the cosmic, ultimate questions of life just leads to more navel-gazing frustration. Our personal journeys, if authentic, will bring us to the large, puzzling questions of life itself. Where do we fit into the scheme of things? Is history going anywhere? Is existence undergirded by an intelligent and loving Source? What are the universal needs of human beings? What satisfies our spiritual restlessness? All inward travelers must eventually face these larger questions.

And finally, if the war is to end between ourselves and the troll, **we** must make the peace initiative. The troll's defensive posture, violent strategies, and hardened cynicism will not allow him to come out from under the bridge and start the negotiations. We will, at times, have to parent the troll. We can listen to him without imitating his violence. We will need a deep and abiding conviction that gentleness is the strongest approach we have. We'll also need a steadfast faith that the troll's woundedness can only be healed by an empathic, loving understanding.

The point, once again, is to accept, own, and embrace the troll rather than make him the enemy we must destroy. Neither ignoring him nor trying to kill him works. When we acknowledge him, and see the hurt beneath his clamoring, we respect ourselves. Honoring ourselves means admitting into full view the entire range of our thoughts however exaggerated they may be, our feelings however turbulent they may be, and our experience however strange it may seem.

"Self-acceptance" means just that. It does not refer to a compulsive, hyperactive desire to get to a different feeling about ourselves. It does not eagerly anticipate how we "will be" after more psychological growth has taken place. It's not constantly looking down the road toward the days in which self-esteem will be born.

Self-acceptance is calm, gentle, assuring, and encouraging. Today, not tomorrow, is where it lives. It knows that where we are today on our individual journey is just as significant as where we will be one year from now, or even ten years from now. It's all part of the path, all necessary for tomorrow to even happen. Where we are **today** is enough. Today, **we** are enough.

7.

Making It Across the Bridge

Crossing the bridge is scary. We're not only facing the troll's inward resistance, but we are also headed for an unfamiliar place. Anxiety, confusion, and uncertainty are definitely part of this process. Yet when we feel extremely anxious, it is often because we are telling ourselves that all uncertainties "should" have been conquered. When we fail to remember the colossal mystery that envelops us, we start pushing ourselves toward greater levels of tension. Our demand for certainty contributes to our uneasiness.

The troll has no respect for the existential questions of life. Confusion has no purpose. Disorientation does not lead us into new realities. In fact, the troll's standard line is, "Oh, grow up!"

The words of philosopher Blaise Pascal, though written over three centuries ago, seem especially relevant for our contemporary problem of anxiety.

> I know not who put me into the world, nor what the world is, nor what I myself am. I am in terrible ignorance of everything. I know not what my body is, nor my senses, nor my soul, not even that part of me which thinks what I say, which reflects on all and on itself, and knows itself no more than the rest. I see those frightful spaces of the universe which surround me, and I find myself tied to one corner of this vast expanse, without knowing why I am put in this place rather than in another, nor why the short time which is given me to live is assigned to me at this point rather than at another of the whole eternity which was before me or which shall come after me.[7]

There is actually something quite humorous about our demand to figure everything out before we go on. When we begin to recognize the multitude of ways we try to escape this dilemma of uncertainty, we see that we're all in the same boat together. Some of us may act as if we know for sure what's going on. The truth, however, is that we don't have the big picture either. Our knowledge, when it comes to ultimate matters, quickly runs out. It is courage which must then take over.

Although uncomfortable, it's important to view anxiety and insecurity as opportunities to grow and understand ourselves. If we are going to suffer, we might as well

60

get something out of it. Why not learn what we can about ourselves, and focus on how the experience is stretching us into people of greater depth? The point, once again, is that bridge-crossing takes courage.

The Courage of Self-Commitment

I once heard a speaker ask a group, "If you were married to yourself, would you stay"? After our smiles disappeared, many of us felt the tug of this question. Would we stay? Is there anything to "stay for?" What do we offer ourselves? What sort of loyalty do we have toward the person we've become? Are we fair, kind, considerate, and protective? Do we offer ourselves an attentive, gracious, gently firm quality of care? Do we make too many demands? Do we have too few expectations? Are we out of balance, alternating back and forth between perfectionism and total sloppiness?

Many of us are not even accustomed to thinking in terms of a "relationship" with ourselves. Even less do we think of having "intimacy" with ourselves. That all sounds very strange. We have relationships with others, not ourselves.

Yet recognizing the significance of this delicate attitude we hold toward ourselves is a step toward new beginnings. We may see ourselves as having been in a fog, a cloak of ignorance concerning the many ways in which we've been neglecting, indulging, over-protecting, or abusing ourselves. More than anything else, a new relationship with ourselves will give us the opportunity to practice gentleness. We will have all sorts of chances to be non-violent. We can develop a rigorous attentiveness and a kind, yet fiercely persistent, loyalty toward our deepest convictions.

Paying Attention Versus Self-Centeredness

Paying attention is not at all the same as being self-centered, selfish, or narcissistic. When we fear the troll, we inevitably become self-absorbed. Being self-absorbed is not our natural condition. It is a by-product of worry. We compulsively twist our focus back on ourselves, miserably assessing whether or not we're okay. Our fears promote greed and an insatiable craving for recognition. We're not designed to sit around wondering if we are adequate. Selfishness and self-centeredness are distortions of a healthy awareness. We're meant to seek beauty, search for truth, laugh with friends, reflect love, and share our experiences. Selfishness and self-centeredness are a sidetrack, a detour away from paying attention.

When we become selfish, we have no idea of our potential for inward abundance. We believe there is not enough attention to go around, so we'd better grab what's available right now! As we narrowly focus on our own wants, we lose interest in life.

We actually become less interesting to ourselves. We cease to envision the inexhaustible resources of compassion and care available. Our self-interests are not really "interesting" at all.

Paying attention means recognizing and respecting our honest thoughts and feelings. This simple act tremendously boosts self-esteem. As we practice treating ourselves with dignity, we begin to cultivate a compassionate disposition toward our own being. This new approach wants to avoid the old malignant patterns and start afresh. We value our own opinions, and we refuse to feel embarrassed by our feelings. We may not act on all those feelings, but we feel no need to ridicule or belittle them.

Bridge-Crossing Signals

How can we know we are crossing the bridge and becoming more self-accepting? We've already seen that there is no magical road map to guide us over the bridge. Nevertheless, are there not trustworthy signs along the way? What are the dependable indicators that we are internalizing grace and not controlled by the troll?

The most obvious signal of growth will be less critical, abusive self-talk and more compassionate, attentive "noticing." It takes a while to make peace with our self-commentary. Demeaning, colorful, violent language may immediately appear when we become frustrated with ourselves. Yet we do not have to take the troll's bait. Blasting ourselves has never produced the change we wanted, so why keep doing it?

"Simply noticing," as Richard Carson has indicated, is a gentle awareness.[8] It is committed to non-violence. In fact, it is based on a vow of non-violence with ourselves. This vow invites more disclosure.

As we experience a more benevolent attentiveness, we will become more spontaneous, expressive, and inwardly free. We will do less editing and censoring of our feelings. We'll lose the sense of "walking on eggs." That self-conscious, rigid, obsessive concern with appearance will start to fade. All of our thoughts, however strange they may appear, will be seen as part of our inward family. We will lose interest in justifying and explaining ourselves to others. And it won't be necessary to analyze everything that swims through us. Our commitment to a nonshaming appreciation of ourselves will involve all that we are.

The energy we poured into self-defense will now be available for other pursuits. We won't have to live our lives on guard. After all, denying, fighting, and avoiding reality involves an immense sacrifice of spontaneity and inward freedom.

We will hide less and share more. Internalized grace will help us more spontaneously reveal who we are. This doesn't mean we will indiscriminately blurt out highly private things, but it does mean we will seek out people around whom we will not be on guard. Our acceptability will no longer be on the line. Remaining in isolation is based on the horrible suspicion of inadequacy. That suspicion, itself, is a troll-created lie. Yet we will learn to be gentle, even with the troll's suspicions. Feeling unacceptable will not necessitate hiding. Discussing our feelings of unacceptability, we will realize, is our best route out of those feelings.

We will also feel less petrified about change. We'll be more willing to risk, even when we're scared. Life will not be perceived as a game in which we make sure we do nothing wrong. Instead, we will be interested in doing things right. William James used to say that there are two types of thinkers: those who chase truth, and those who dodge error.[9] Our willingness to risk will invite, rather than shrink away from, change and process. The bridge will be less intimidating.

Because of decreased defensiveness and a new-found energy, we will have a greater sense of curiosity, interest, and aliveness. Childlike qualities will return. The numbness, fatigue, and boredom associated with rigid self-defense will pale. We will "become as little children" in many ways. Just as children have a profound ability to become interested in things, so we will rediscover this capacity.

We'll have greater trust in our own experiencing and thinking. The self-doubts, when they appear, won't be as paralyzingly negative. We will understand that we can live with doubt. Trusting our own perceptions will not mean refusing to check things out with other people's reality. But it will mean refusing to immediately abandon our own perspective. The self-belittling, "other-people-must-know-more-than-I-know" tendency will begin to dissolve.

We will also have a growing conviction that inner resources and friendly support will be available as we face our difficulties and uncertainties. Our image of providence may not involve a magical manipulation of events, but it will involve a quiet trust that redemptive possibilities accompany any turbulence we have to face. We will not be left completely alone with our unaided efforts. We will learn to trust the future. We will be less paranoid about outside help. Aware of the risks, we will still open our hearts to life.

We'll be less willing to wear a mask. Non-violently, we'll insist on being ourselves. More and more, we will realize that if other people find our genuineness intolerable, then it is their problem, not ours. This is not an aggressive, or necessarily even a rebellious, attitude. It simply recognizes that we have only one life in which to be real. Time is passing quickly. If people like or love only a false appearance of who we are, then what will we have gained? Selling our birthright for a bowl of approval is just not worth it. We have the right to be the person we are. In fact, it is a sacred privilege. When others attempt to rob us of the opportunity to express the singular, unique variety of humanness that is us, we **need** to become angry. The anger need not be violent, but it certainly needs to be self-protective.

The ability to find the appropriate sources of acceptance and nurture will leave us with less need to win everyone else's approval. We'll see the need for "everyone's" approval as a childish fantasy. Our stomachs will not rise into our throats when we hear a disapproving comment. We won't have to react. It will simply be all right for others to think what they think. In fact, we won't feel a need to control their liking or disliking us. This new-found freedom will be a wonderful gift of grace.

Being gentle with ourselves will also mean being gentle with our past. We'll need to put the events of our lives in historical perspective. We'll also need a compassionate re-tracing of our steps, not a judgmental account of our errors. Most of the time, we did the best we could do under the circumstances. We had limited resources. We didn't know what we know now. It's not fair for us to judge yesterday's reality by today's standards. It's sometimes easy to fall into a self-righteous attitude toward our earlier struggles.

Connected to this, there will be less rehearsal of past mistakes. Recycling "wrong turns" will not be the way we interpret our lives. Instead, we will see mere outcomes from which we can either lament or grow. Mistakes, as teachers, are reminders of human limits. They are sometimes painful. But the only tragedy is refusing to learn from them, not making them. They simply supply us with feedback that a particular move was not wise. That's information we need. If we had done nothing, we wouldn't have that information.

As we become more gentle with ourselves, that same gentleness will spill over onto others. We will become less judgmental, less condemning, and less interested in gossip. The best guarantee against judging others is becoming more acceptant of ourselves. Harsh condemnation of others indicates an unfamiliarity with our own inner worlds. When we see our own potential for unhealthy and destructive behavior, we will be less shocked and appalled by others' behavior. We'll come down from our pedestals and recognize our common human frailties. We'll no longer pretend that someone else's behavior is "simply unthinkable" to us. We'll begin to digest the words of Oscar Wilde, "All of us are in the gutter. It's just that some of us are looking up at the stars."[10]

The more we understand that self-judgment and condemnation have done nothing for us, the less prone we'll be to dish it out for others. We'll simply lose interest in evaluating and criticizing people. We will see the woundedness and pain underneath the unhealthy habits. Further, we'll see the distorted desire for wholeness beneath the disturbed acts. In short, we'll look with greater depth. We'll better understand the frustrated needs and inward void that lead to self-destructive behavior.

Gentleness will resist the convenience of black-and-white categories. We are too complex for easy right/wrong, good/bad categories. These dichotomies do not respect the mystery of our being. We aren't saints or sinners, completely altruistic or totally selfish, absolutely misguided or perfectly accurate. These all-or-nothing categories are not flexible enough to interpret our lives. In fact, it is an act of violence to force our experience to fit these rigid polarities.

We will also begin to appreciate the ordinary events and routines of our lives, and feel less need for highly dramatic, sensational experience. With greater self-acceptance, we'll bring more of ourselves into each moment. As we experience the present with greater awareness, it will become more alive and exciting. For instance, when we talk with a friend, we'll **talk** with a friend; when we listen to music, we'll **hear** the music; when we drive a car, we'll **drive** the car. In other words, we will participate, with much more awareness, in what we're doing. Put simply, we'll take our awareness with us when we go somewhere.

This is a marked difference from the way many of us have lived. We've been half into conversations, unaware of what we're eating, and thinking about the laundry while we watch a movie. We relive past events or think about next week's problems. We spend little time in "now," and then wonder why our lives are boring or even depressing. But when we self-acceptantly bring ourselves into an experience, the experience takes on a new significance. It's like going from a black-and-white to a color screen.

Making ourselves psychologically available will be a disciplined act of love. It will be love for ourselves, as well as love for the person with whom we are sharing an experience. The mere act of focusing on what someone is saying will communicate enormous respect and care for them. They will feel valued. This simple gesture will promote feelings of dignity.

And finally, we'll have less need for magic, and more acceptance that self-esteem is an ongoing process. It is not an ecstatic event or a "once-in-a-lifetime" experience. It is a gradual process of renewing our commitment toward the person we are.

Grace That Leads Us Home

The New Testament story of the prodigal son is also the story of our relationship with the troll. Disconnected from the wandering, lonely, insecure part of our identity, we ponder why we feel depressed, "half here," sad, abandoned, and dull. Life often feels bland, uneventful, and painfully divided. Struggling with this estrangement, or internal separation, we yearn for a unifying experience. We want to feel whole again and "together."

Yet, in spite of our yearning for at-one-ment, several spiritual and psychological traditions remind us that **we can't come home alone**. We may relentlessly attempt to achieve self-acceptance in isolation. We may want to stay disconnected from people while we journey across the bridge. But somewhere along the way, someone has to mediate an acceptance that we can't find on our own. All individual healing begins in the context of an accepting relationship. Without this help, we cannot "get out from under" our own sense of condemnation. This help may have come from our first therapist, a non-judgmental friend, a compassionate minister, or anyone else. The point is that it was offered.

This inability to psychologically "save ourselves" is part of our limits as a human being. We cannot muscle up the individual strength to pull ourselves out of a sense of inadequacy. As we have seen, there are no successful fix-it-at-home kits. It won't work alone. We cannot give ourselves what we do not have. The troll is too strong.

Even pioneers of the human potential movement, such as Carl Rogers, recognized that self-acceptance is born out of being in an accepting relationship. Self-acceptance is not something we can accomplish as an act of the will. An accepting relationship is initially necessary to deliver us from our distorted self-perceptions, fears, and shame.

Human beings are capable of enormous self-doubt. In isolation, the message of grace often cannot reach us. Grace must be mediated, passed on indirectly, and given concrete form. Many times, the abstract, hypothetical notion of "acceptability" is not very plausible to us. Further, vague notions of our acceptance are not transforming. Joseph Cooke puts this point beautifully.

> ...if we happen to be in a situation where no single living person really knows us, or loves us just as we are, or reaches out to give of himself to meet our needs, it is almost impossible to find very much meaning in the idea of God's acceptance. The grace is all theoretical—off in the fantasy world of wish fulfillment or empty intellectualization. But the legalism, the non-grace, the sense of worthlessness and rejection are real. They are what we experience and live with every day. It's hard to rest in God's uncondemning love and acceptance if we feel that the people around us are ignoring us, condemning us, criticizing us, putting us down. If grace is to mean anything to us, it has to have feet that run to meet us, hands that reach out to us, eyes that see us, a mouth that speaks to us, a heart that loves us and cares what happens to us. [11]

We need to see a piece of our acceptability in a friend's smile, learn to trust ourselves as we are treated with dignity, and recognize our own value as we are offered a compassionate respect. Again, others were involved in our getting lost; others will also be involved in our finding home.

We can't come home until we know it's safe. Finding that sacred place within ourselves requires a non-threatening atmosphere and the promise of no judgment. Compassion and love pull back the curtain of our self-understanding. Grace is necessary for us to take the plunge into who we are. We need to know "ahead of time" that it's going to be okay. We are then free to explore, risk, and find out what we're about. We must have this deep assurance that we are acceptable no matter what we "dig up."

Most of us live with anticipations of judgment. Previous experiences of being ridiculed, exposed, or shamed have set us up to be leery. We shy away from where we're not welcome, and we withhold our secrets when we smell rejection. Grace opens the gates to self-discovery.

We need to know that others have been lost, too. We have a deep need to know that others have felt our sense of desperation, self-doubt, and anxiety. Otherwise, their hope is just another form of cheap consolation. We need to hear and feel connected to their stories. We need to know they've suffered as we have. Did they bleed as we did? Was their path also directionless and without purpose? They must know, as we have known, what despair feels, smells, and tastes like. Have they felt like a stranger to both themselves and others? We need this human connection of being lost if "finding home" is to mean anything.

We cannot "find home" unless we have left home. "Home" is not that safe, secure, familiar identity bestowed upon us by our families. Our families may have provided much nurture, care, and excellent tools for a solid foundation. Yet our path is not their path. Authentic spirituality always insists that our faith truly be **our** faith.

It is very easy to cling to familiar patterns and dodge the more frightening quest for our own sense of self. Sometimes, people who care deeply for us can pull us away from our own direction. The gospel of Matthew mentions that our "enemies" will often be members of our own household. This is not a deliberately malicious act on the part of family members. They simply may not understand what we're experiencing. They may feel threatened by our lack of conformity. Yet finding home, in all the great religious traditions, necessitates leaving this safe, comfortable world.

We may be led home by unexpected people. The experience of grace is not predictable. Nothing is "off limits." Mirrors of our acceptability can come from almost any source. This makes life rich with possibilities. We often expect our "sacred core" to be mirrored through a "holy" person or an expert in the people business. Yet our acceptability may be most powerfully reflected in a child's words, the comments of a man picking up our trash, or the kindness of a rushed waitress taking our order. The deepest truths about us can emerge in unlikely places and from unexpected sources.

I remember going to a small hospital one evening to do an educational program for staff members. As I walked toward one of the doors of the hospital, I saw a young girl sitting on a curb in front of the emergency room entrance. She was petting a small cat. This girl could not possibly have been over ten years old. Feeling cheerful, I approached her. "Is that your cat?" I asked. "No" she replied. "I wonder how old it is," I said. "I don't know," she replied. "Wonder if it's a girl or boy," I responded. "I don't know," she said. "Wonder what neighborhood it's from?" I continued. "I don't know," she said, rather annoyed. "I wonder if it has a family around," I asked. She looked at me and responded, "I don't know...Is that important to you?" I walked into the hospital with a smile on my face.

I found a tremendous lesson about grace in this simple interaction. I was interested in categorizing, labeling, and identifying this cat. I brought up all sorts of conditional factors about how old it was, whether it was male/female, what sort of neighborhood it was from, whether it came from a concerned family, and so on. The little girl was interested in only one thing: Here was a cat that looked as though it needed some affection. All the other factors were irrelevant. Those other issues may have been "important to me" but they interrupted the flow of grace. It is often in unexpected situations such as this that we learn deep truths about the nature of grace.

Home is the source of compassion and gratitude. When we find "home," we want to help others find "home." This is the way grace affects us. It triggers gratitude and a desire to "give back to life" some of the wealth within us. "Home" provides an abundance of compassion, with plenty to go around. We can tap this source again and again, even when we feel exhausted.

This "grace that leads us home" often meets us in our deepest hour of woundedness. When the voices of not being enough are strongest, a gentle acceptance often appears. I have read no more powerful description of this experience than Paul Tillich's classic statement about how grace comes into our lives.

Grace strikes us when we are in great pain and restlessness. It strikes us when we walk through the dark valley of a meaningless and empty life. It strikes us when we feel that our separation is deeper than usual, because we have violated another life, a life which we loved, or from which we were estranged. It strikes us when our own disgust for our own being, our indifference, our weakness, our hostility, and our lack of direction and composure have become intolerable to us. It strikes us when, year after year, the longed-for perfection of life does not appear, when the old compulsions reign within us as they have for decades, when despair destroys all joy and courage. Sometimes at that moment a wave of light breaks into our darkness, and it is as though a voice were saying: "You are accepted. You are accepted, accepted by that which is greater than you, and the name of which you do not know. Do not ask for the name now; perhaps you will find it later. Do not try to do anything now; perhaps later you will do much. Do not seek for anything; do not perform anything; do not intend anything. Simply accept the fact that you are accepted!" If that happens to us, we experience grace.[12]

May you and your troll find such grace.

Notes

1. Thomas Oden, **The Structure of Awareness**. Nashville: Abingdon, 1969.

2. Karen Horney, **Our Inner Conflicts**. New York: W.W. Norton, 1945.

3. Paul Tillich, **The Shaking of the Foundations**. New York: Scribner's, 1948, p. 59.

4. Robert Louis Stevenson, **Dr. Jekyll and Mr. Hyde**. New York: Bantam, 1981.

5. Theodore I. Rubin, **Compassion and Self-Hate**. New York: David McKay, Inc., 1975, p. 32.

6. Thomas Oden, op. cit.

7. Blaise Pascal, **Pensées**. New York: Modern Library, 1941, p. 68.

8. Richard Carson, **Taming Your Gremlin**. New York: Perennial Library, 1968.

9. William James, "The Will to Believe," in John J. McDermott (ed.), **The Writings of William James**. New York: Modern Library, 1968.

10. Quoted in F. Forrester Church, **Everyday Miracles**. New York: Warner Books, 1988, p. 158.

11. Joseph R. Cooke, **Free for the Taking**. Old Tappan: Fleming H. Revell, 1975, p. 184.

12. Paul Tillich, op. cit., pp. 161-162.